BOWIE

A MICHAEL ALLRED COLORING BOOK

Based on the unauthorized graphic biography
BOWIE: Stardust, Rayguns & Moonage Daydreams

Co-written by Michael Allred and Steve Horton, and originally colored by Laura Allred

INSIGHT
EDITIONS

San Rafael • Los Angeles • London

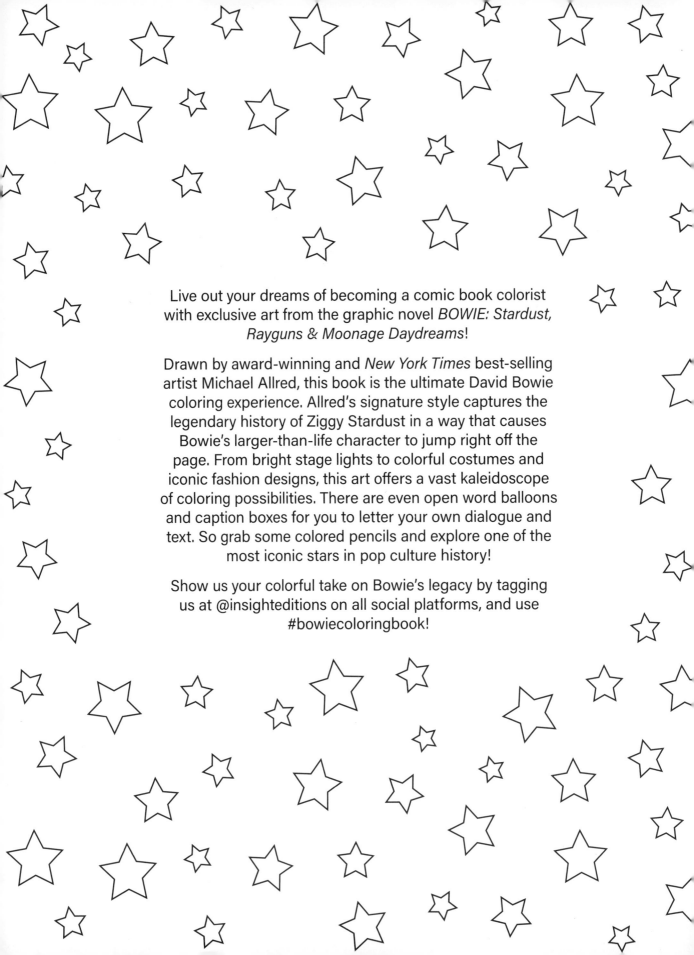

Live out your dreams of becoming a comic book colorist with exclusive art from the graphic novel *BOWIE: Stardust, Rayguns & Moonage Daydreams*!

Drawn by award-winning and *New York Times* best-selling artist Michael Allred, this book is the ultimate David Bowie coloring experience. Allred's signature style captures the legendary history of Ziggy Stardust in a way that causes Bowie's larger-than-life character to jump right off the page. From bright stage lights to colorful costumes and iconic fashion designs, this art offers a vast kaleidoscope of coloring possibilities. There are even open word balloons and caption boxes for you to letter your own dialogue and text. So grab some colored pencils and explore one of the most iconic stars in pop culture history!

Show us your colorful take on Bowie's legacy by tagging us at @insighteditions on all social platforms, and use #bowiecoloringbook!

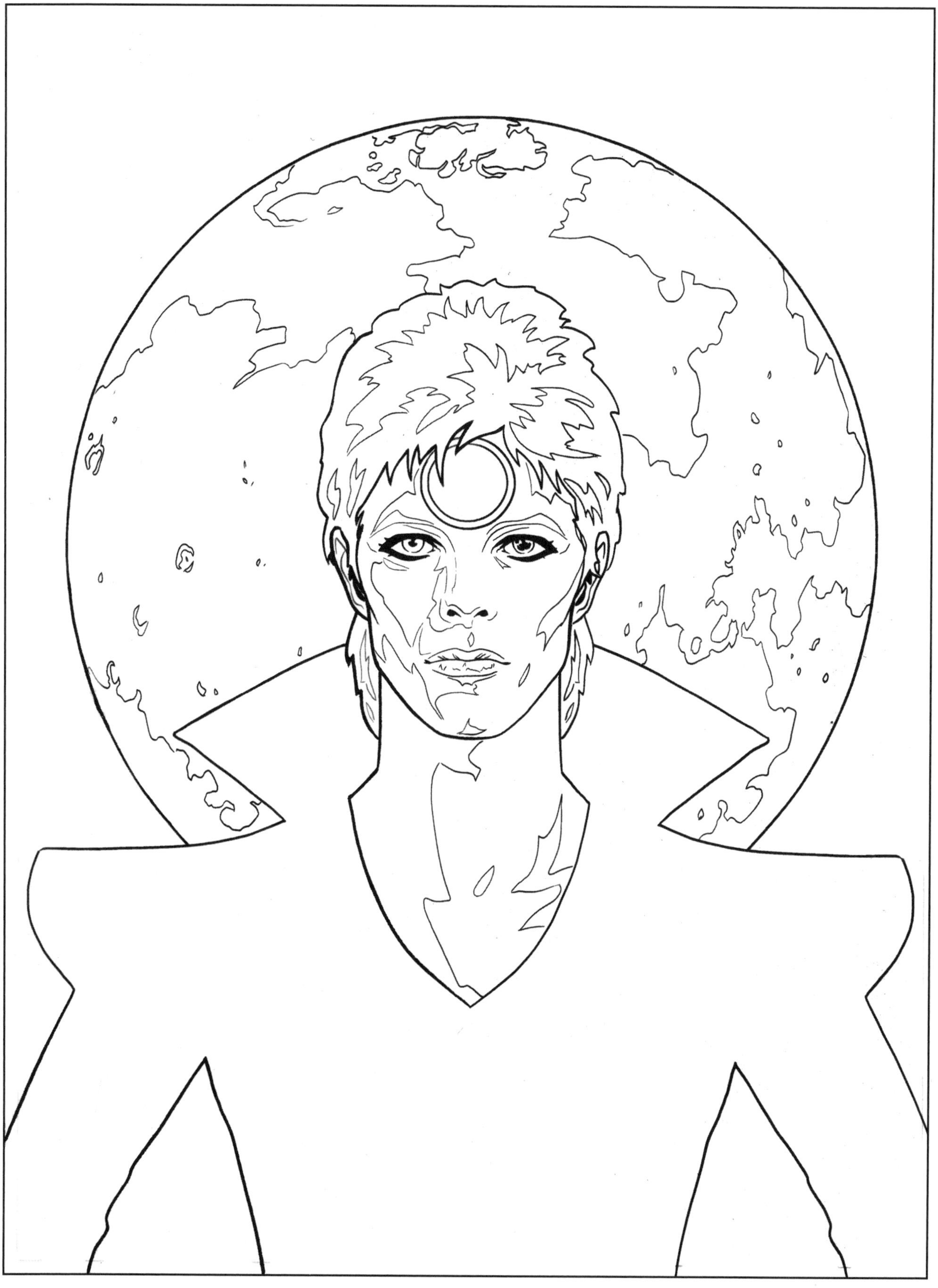

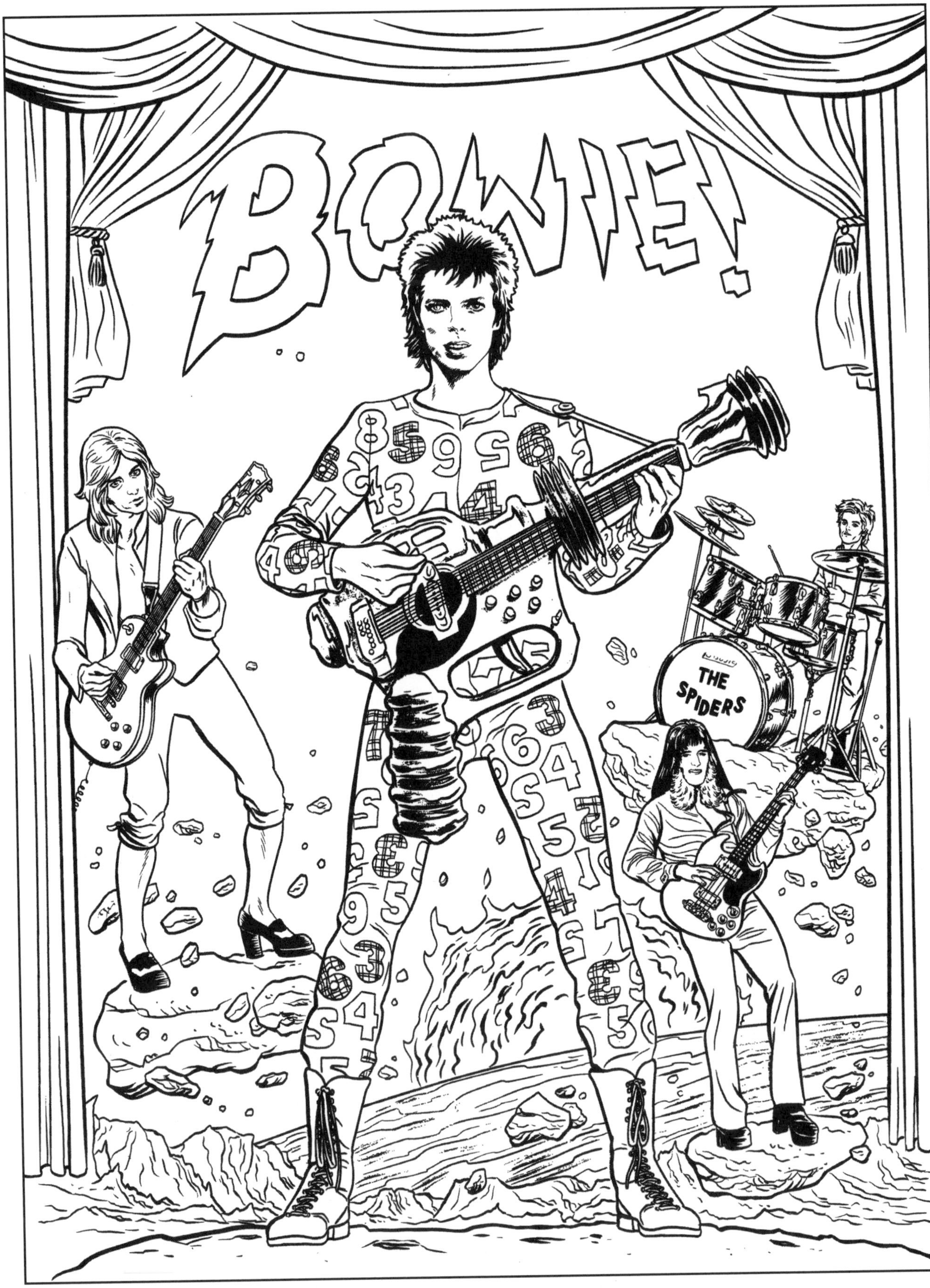
BOWIE!
THE SPIDERS

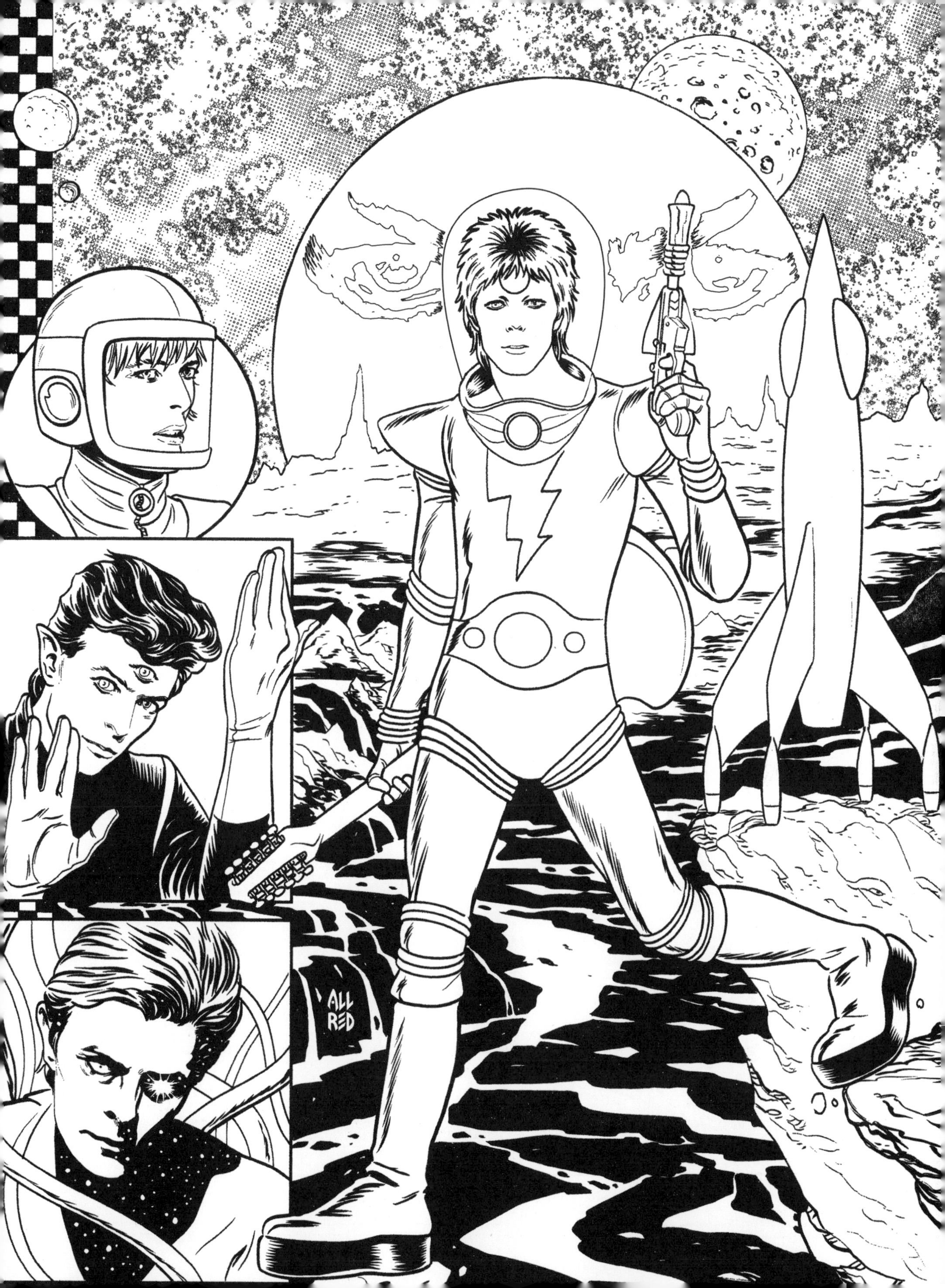
ALL
RED

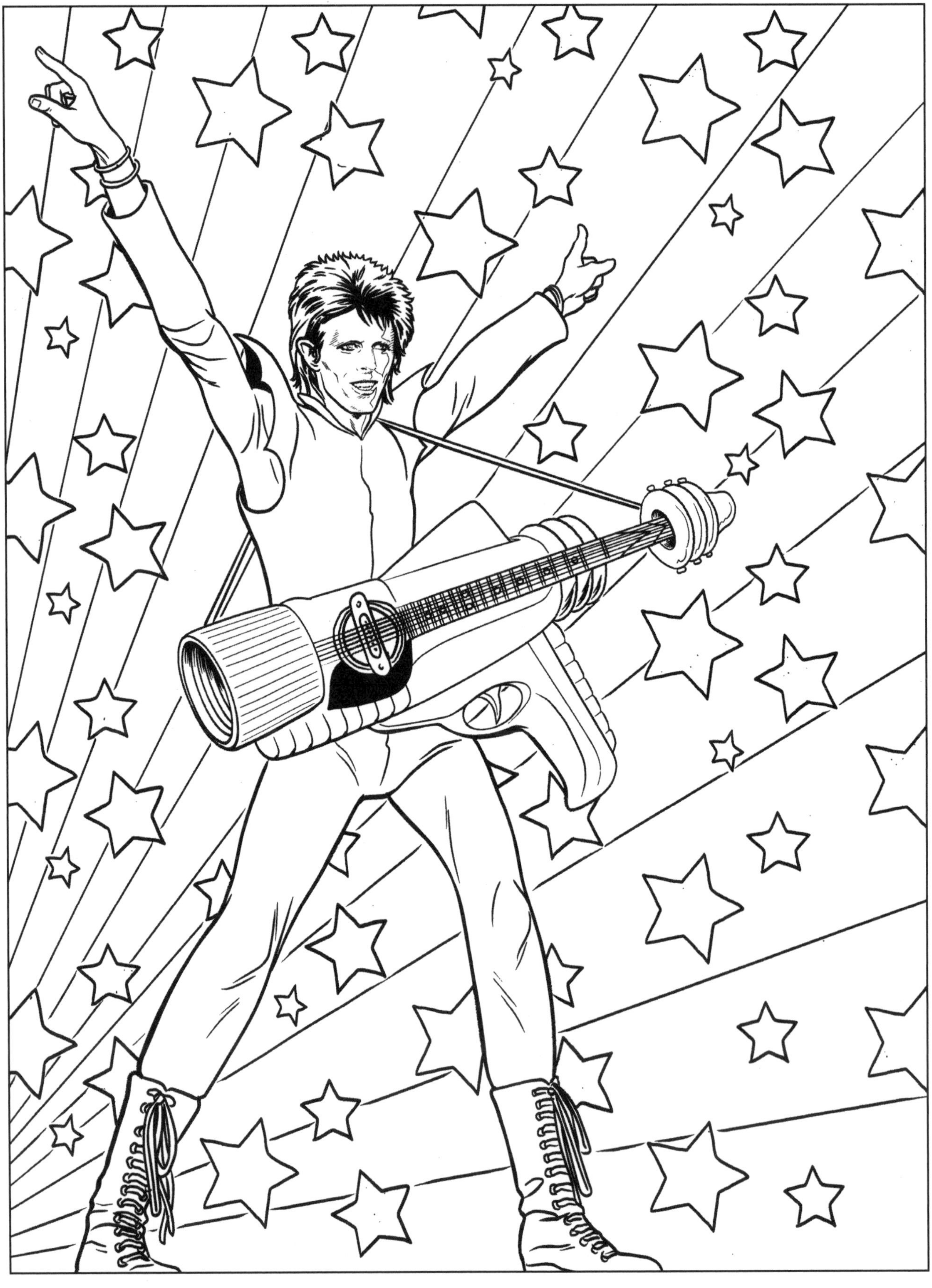

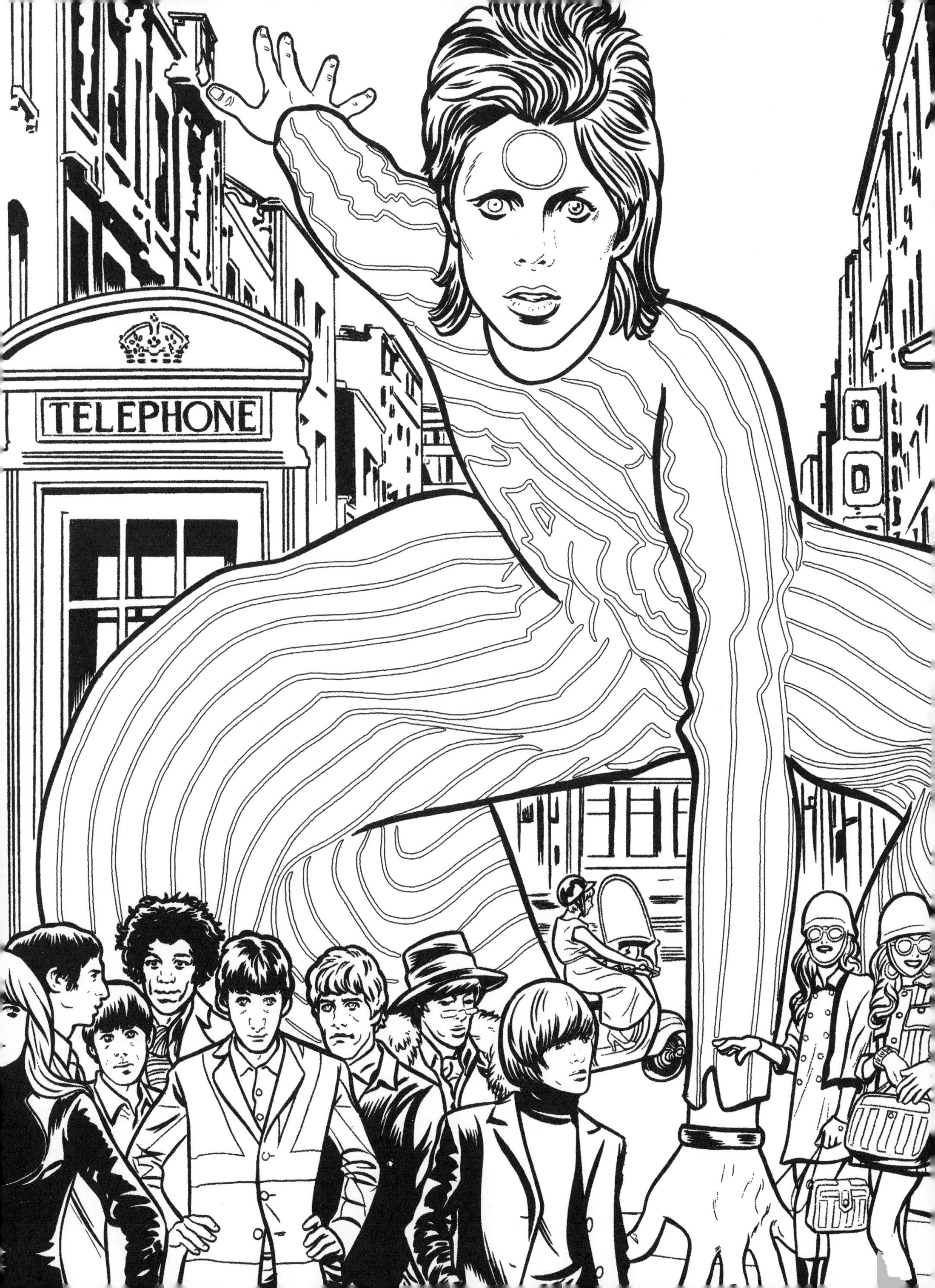
TELEPHONE

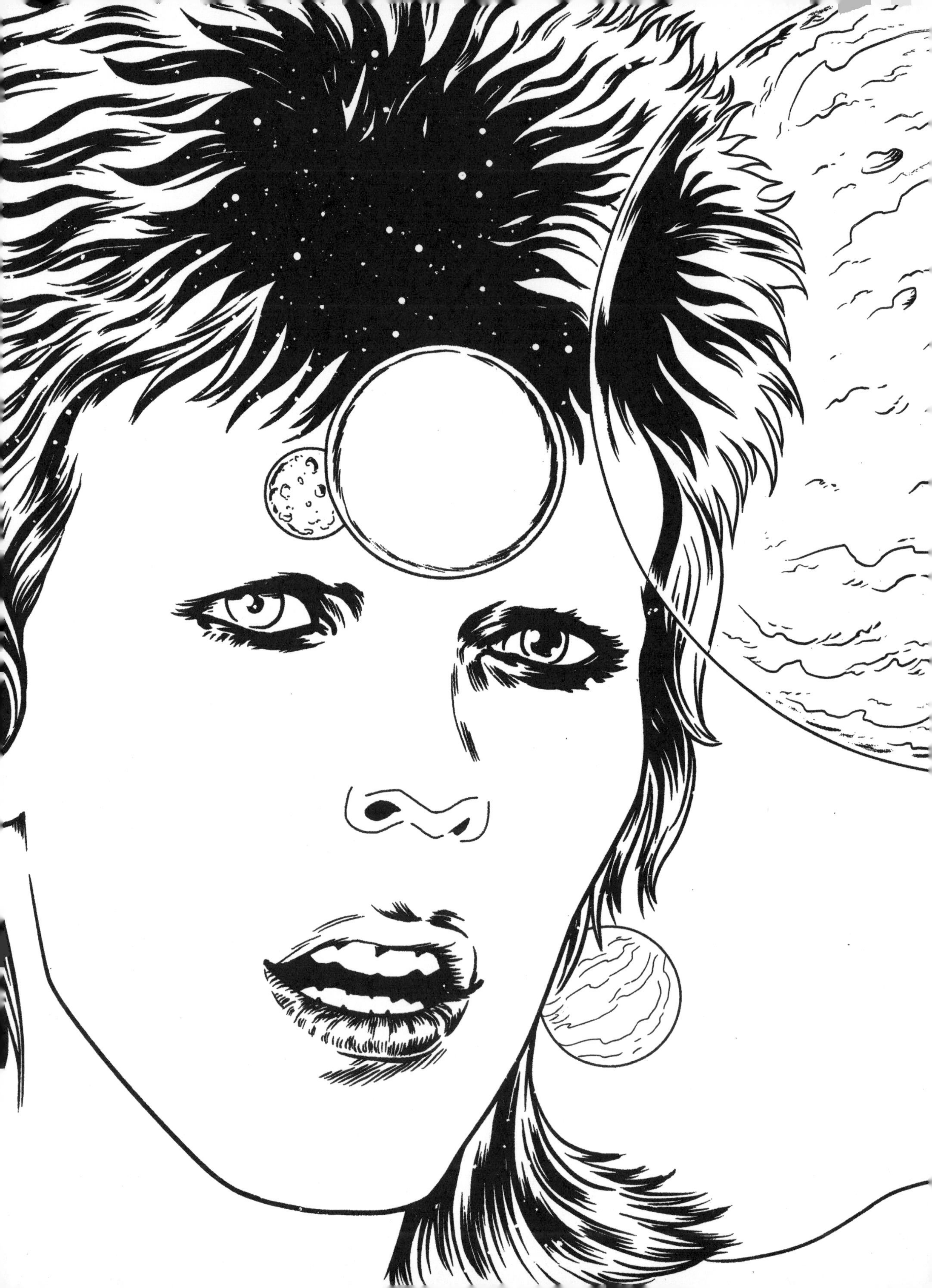

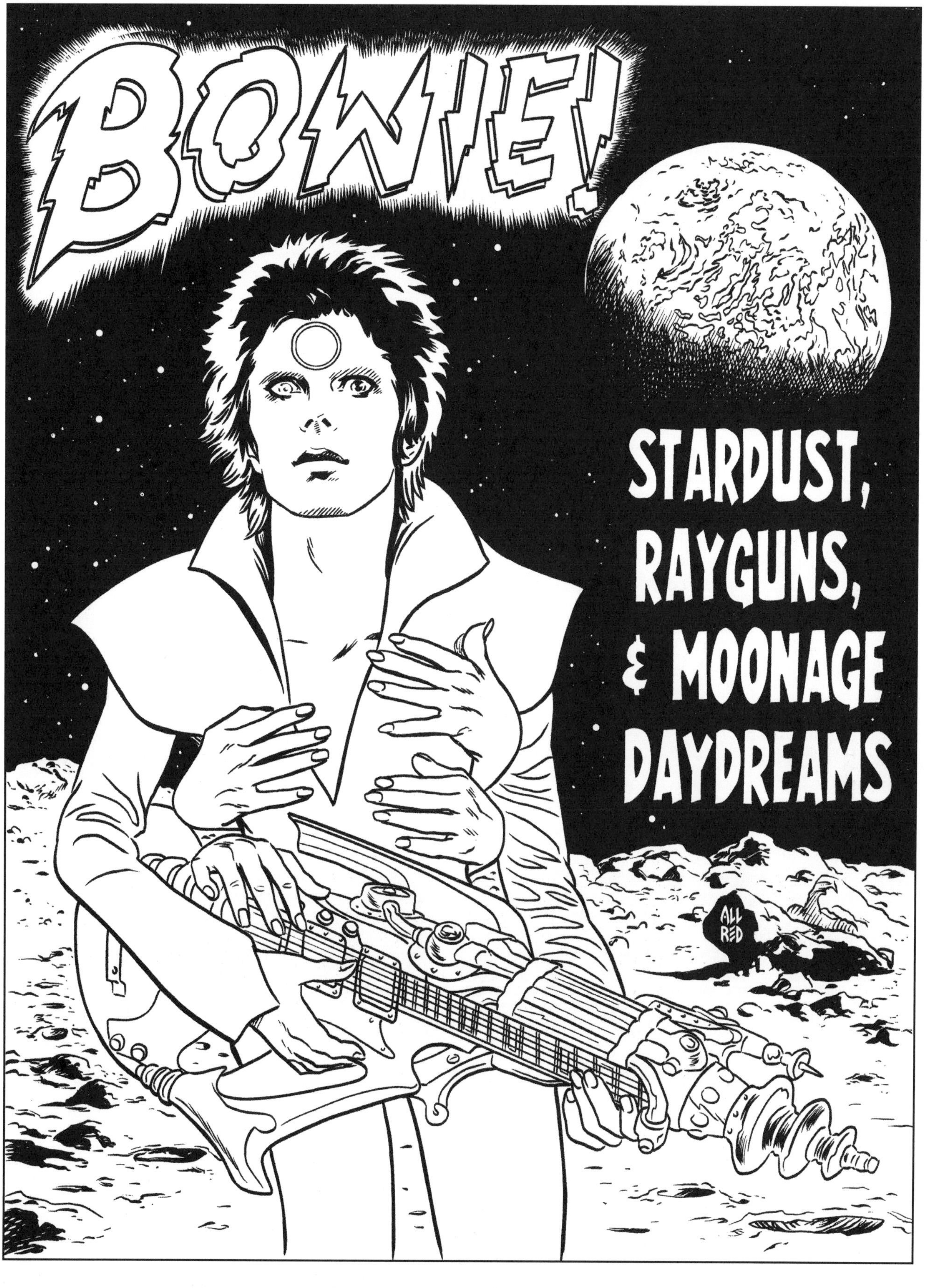
BOWIE!
STARDUST,
RAYGUNS,
& MOONAGE
DAYDREAMS
ALLRED

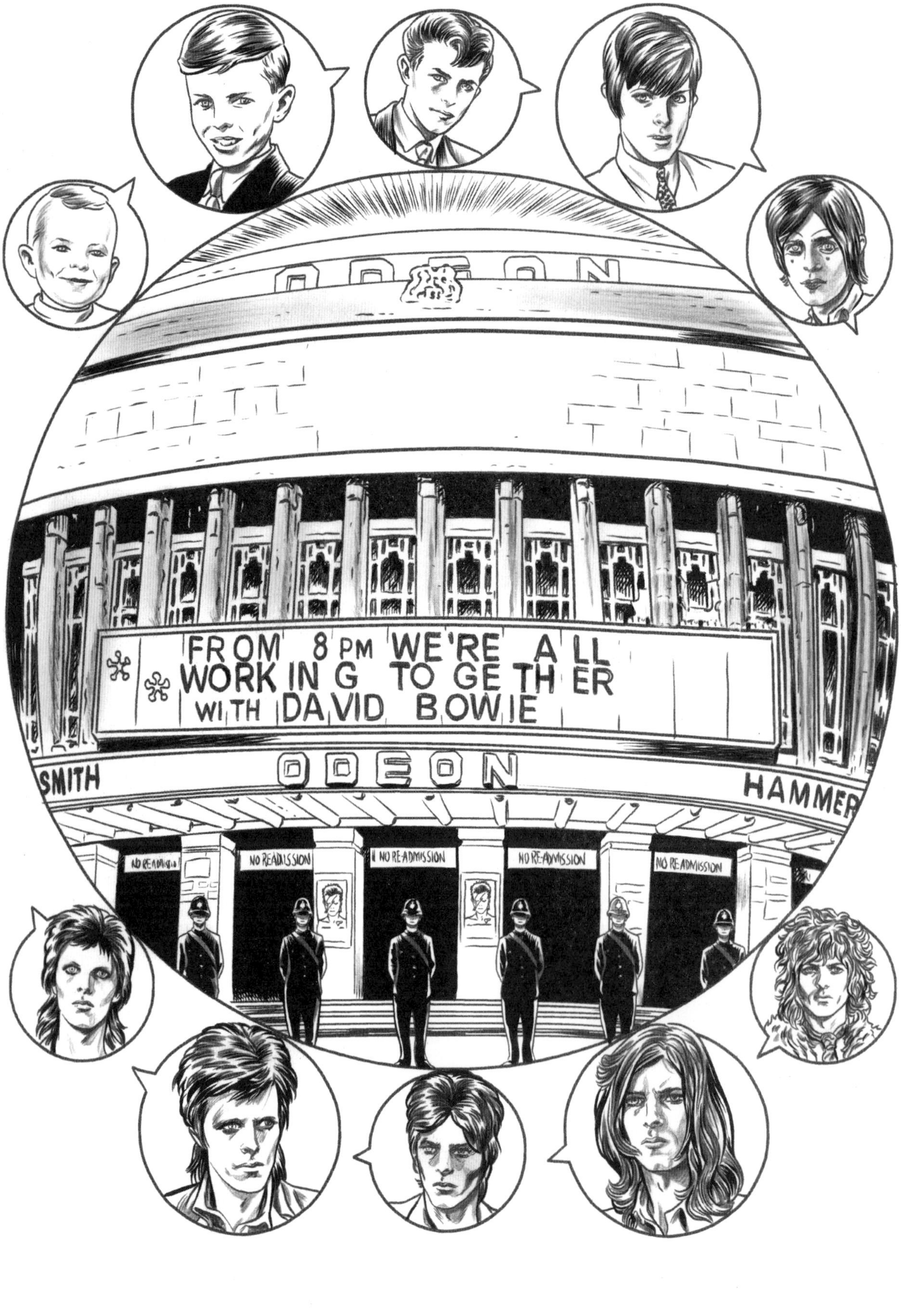
FROM 8 PM WE'RE ALL
WORKING TOGETHER
WITH DAVID BOWIE
ODEON
SMITH
HAMMER
NO RE-ADMISSION
NO RE-ADMISSION
NO RE-ADMISSION
NO RE-ADMISSION

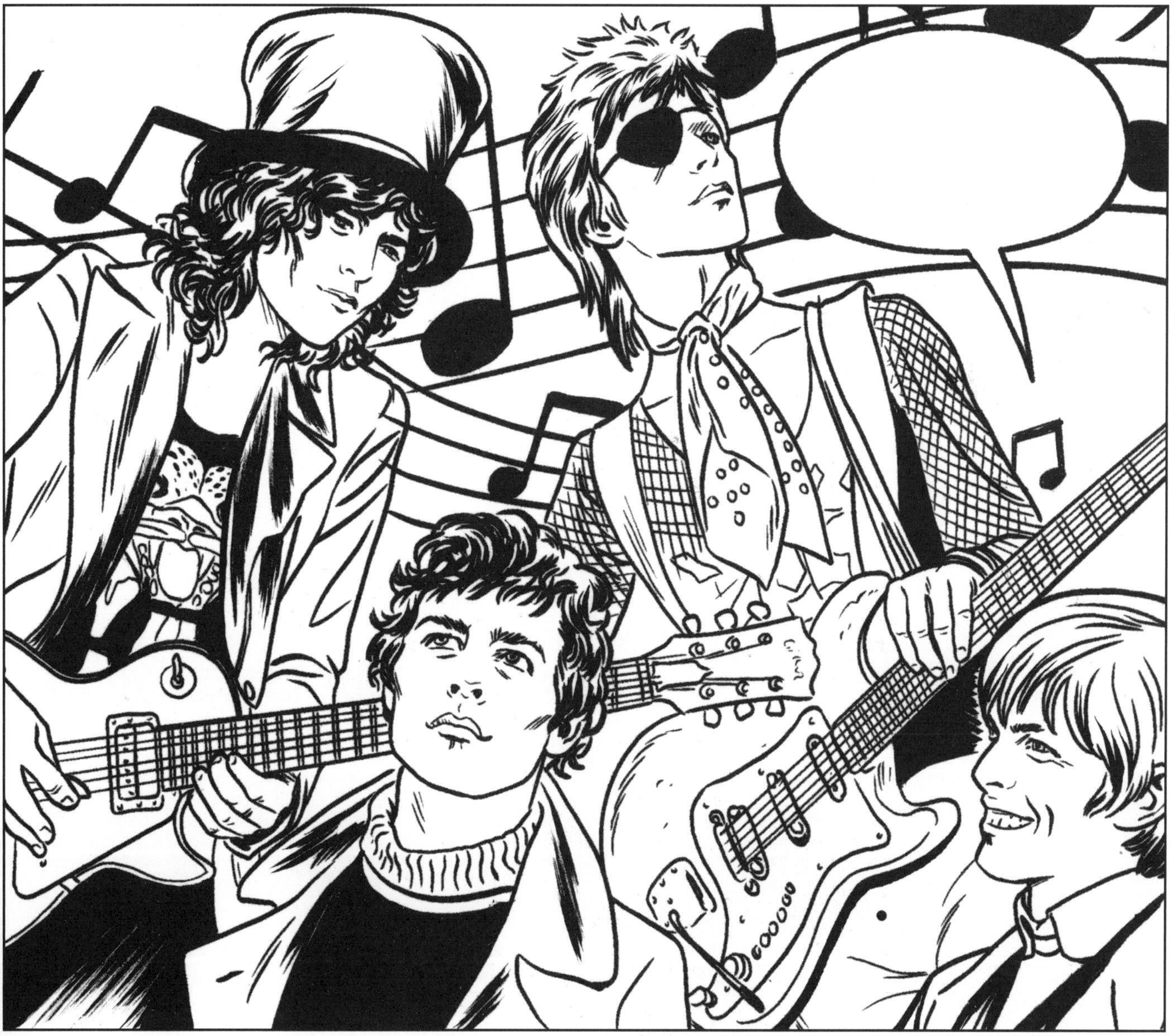

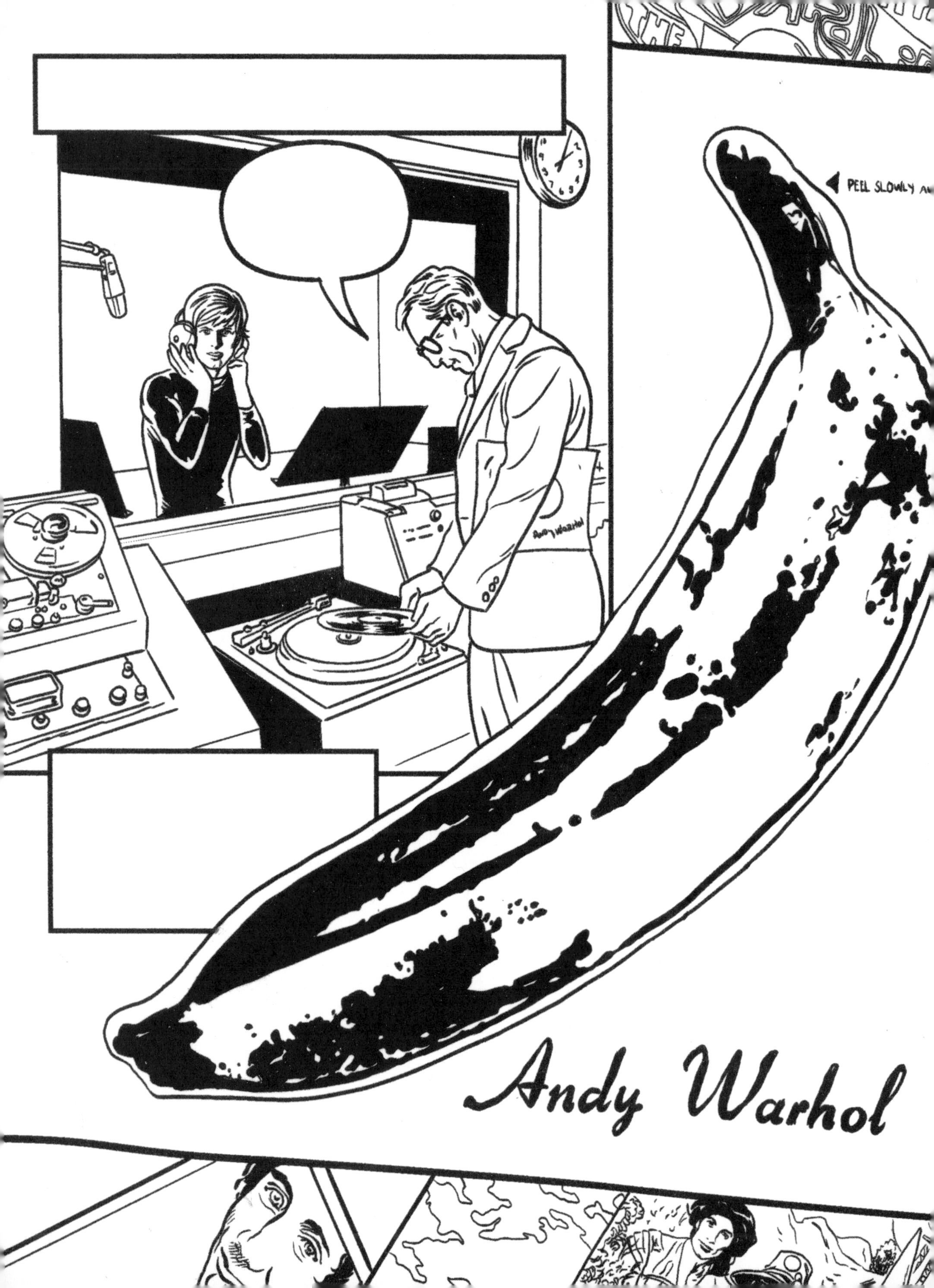
PEEL SLOWLY
Andy Warhol

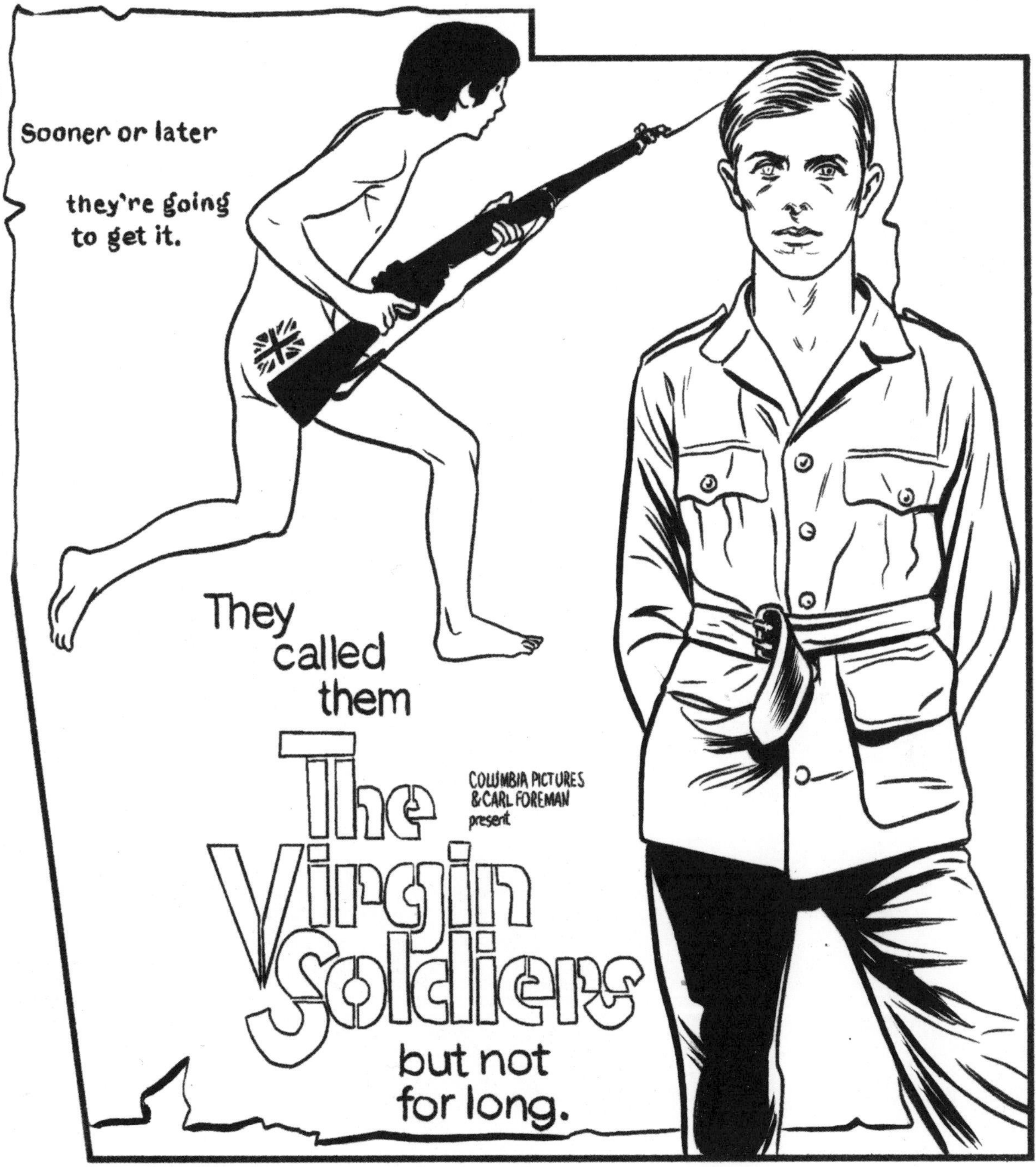
Sooner or later
they're going to get it.
They called them
The Virgin Soldiers
COLUMBIA PICTURES
& CARL FOREMAN
present
but not for long.

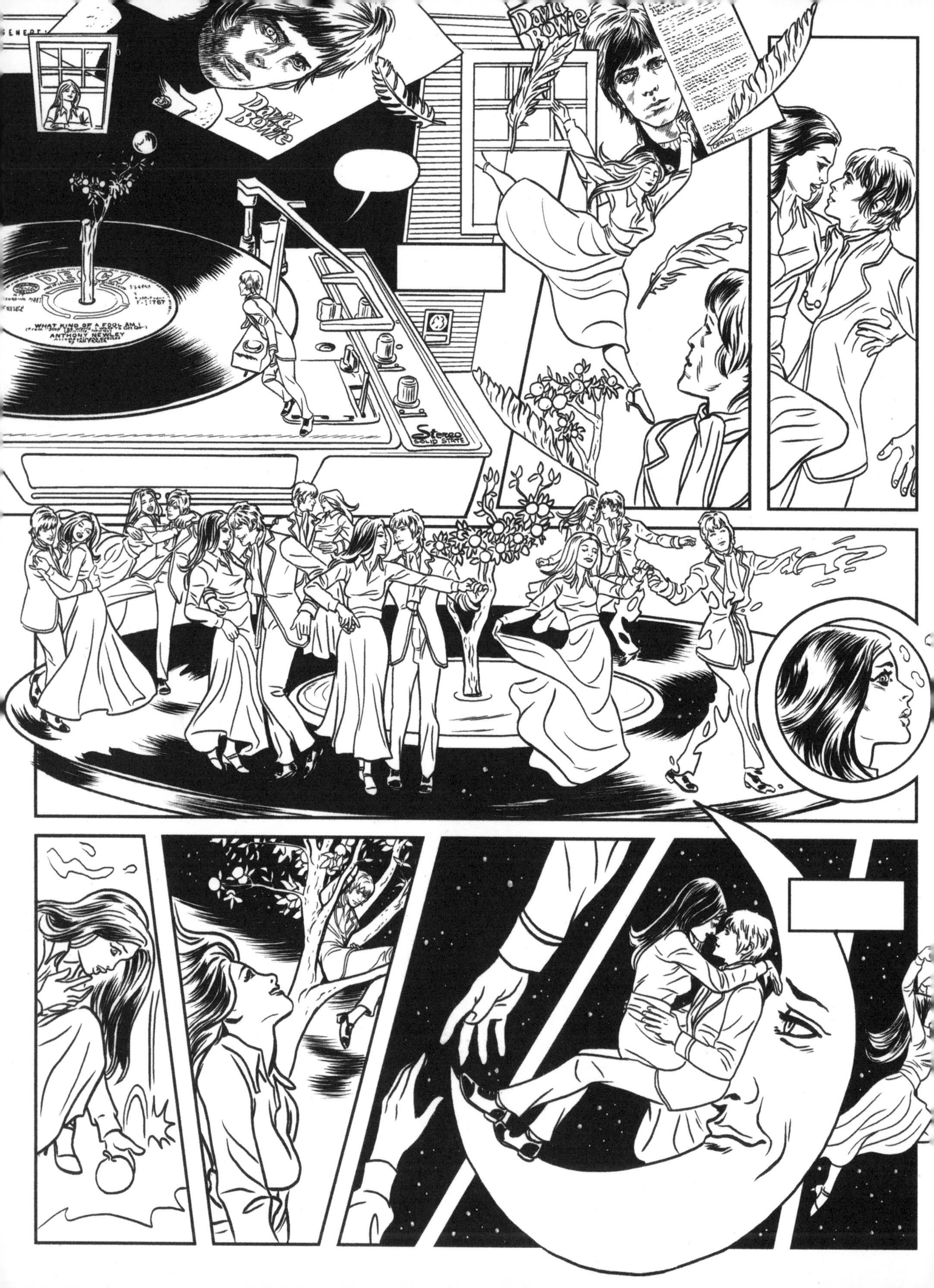
David Bowie
DECCA
WHAT KIND OF A FOOL AM I
ANTHONY NEWLEY
Stereo
SOLID STATE
David Bowie

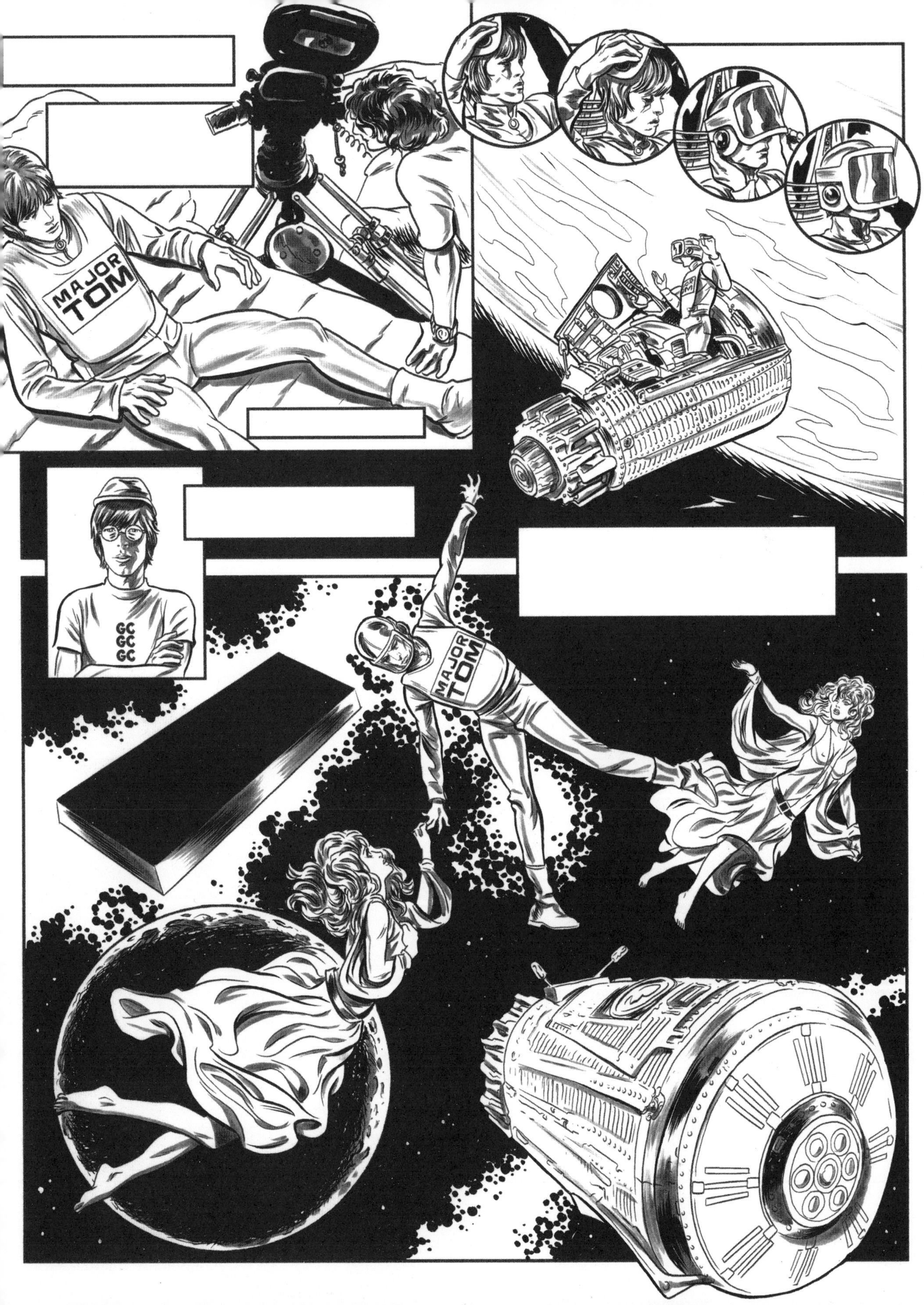
MAJOR TOM
GC GC GC
MAJOR TOM

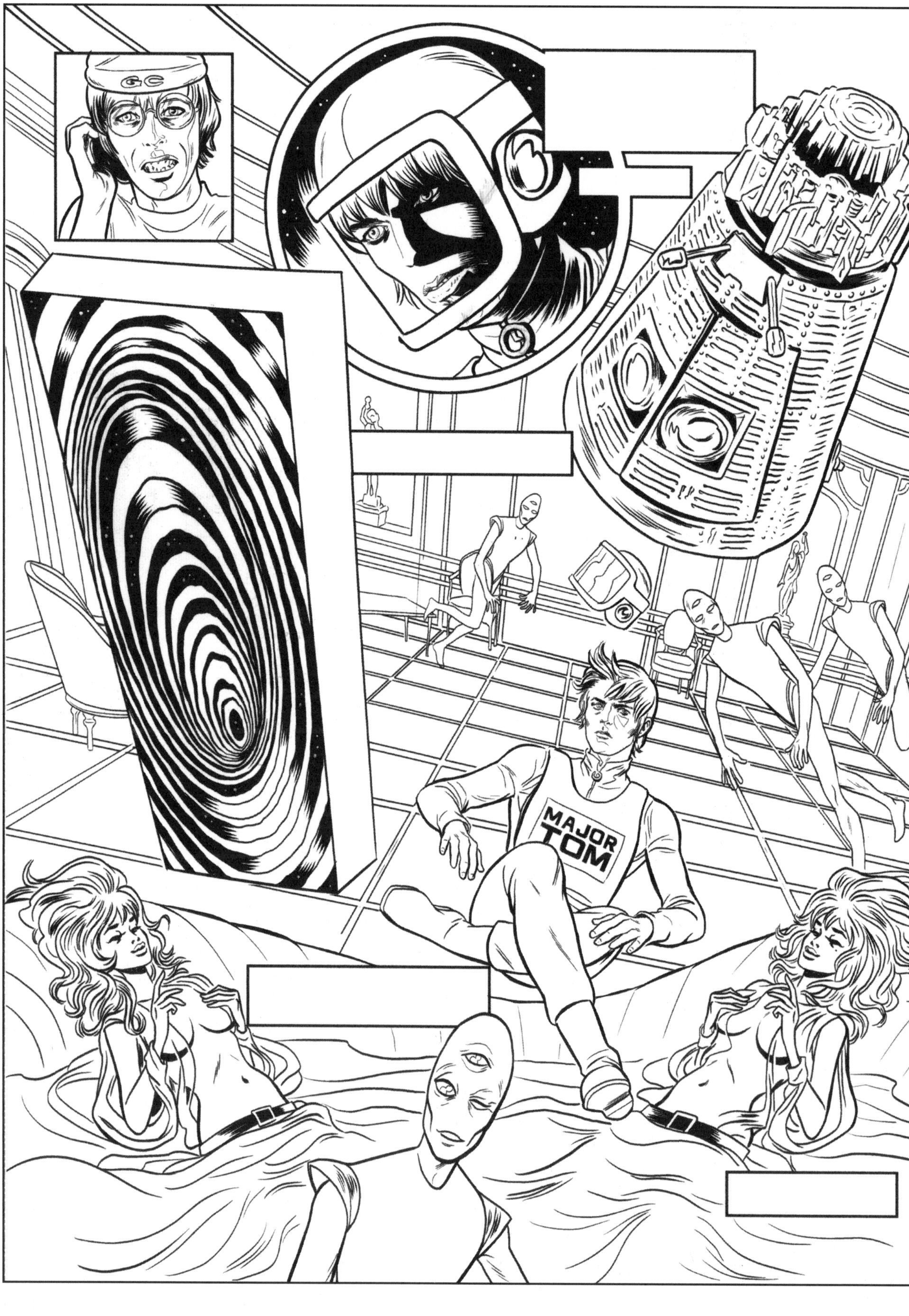
GC
MAJOR TOM

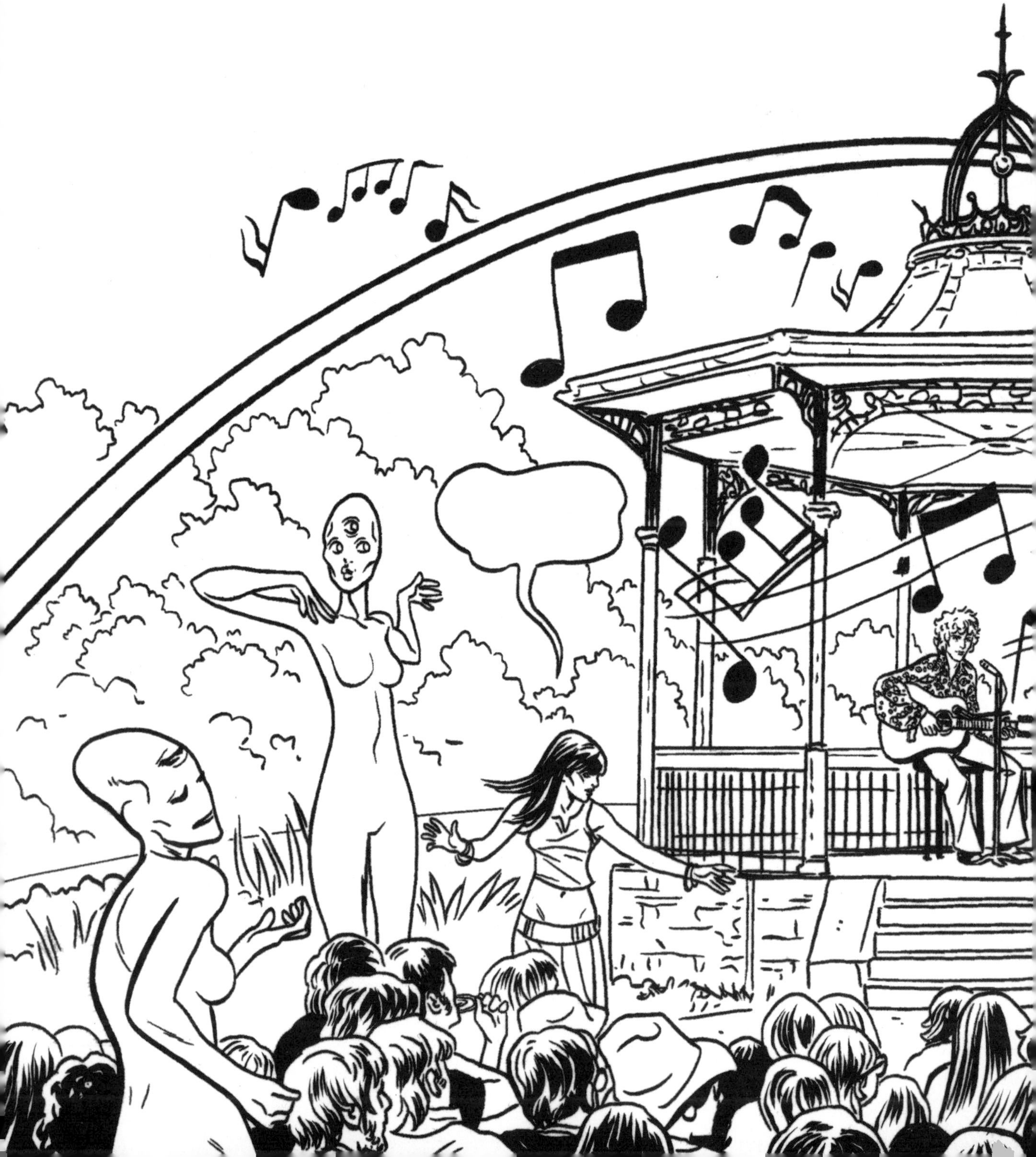

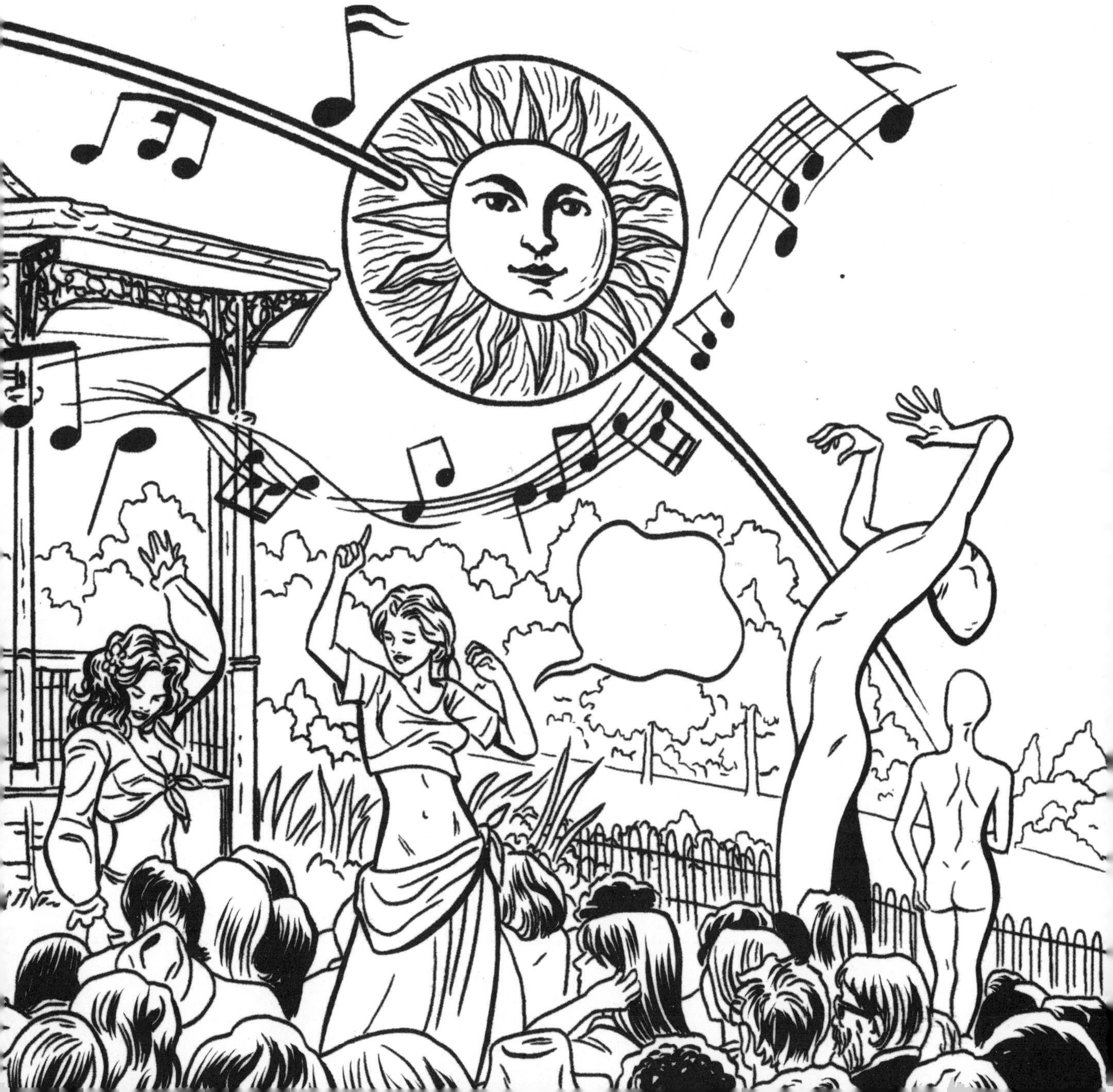

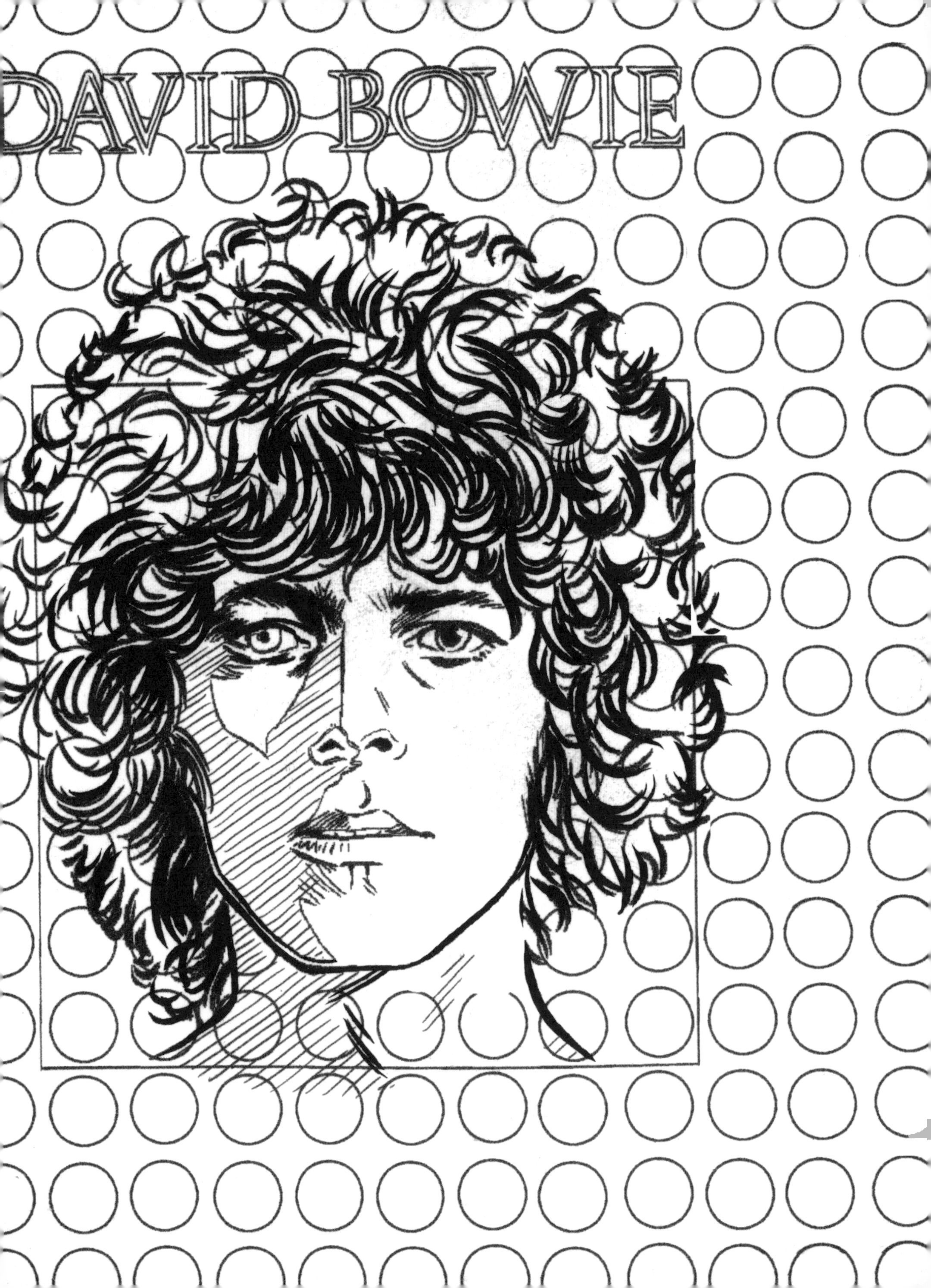
DAVID BOWIE

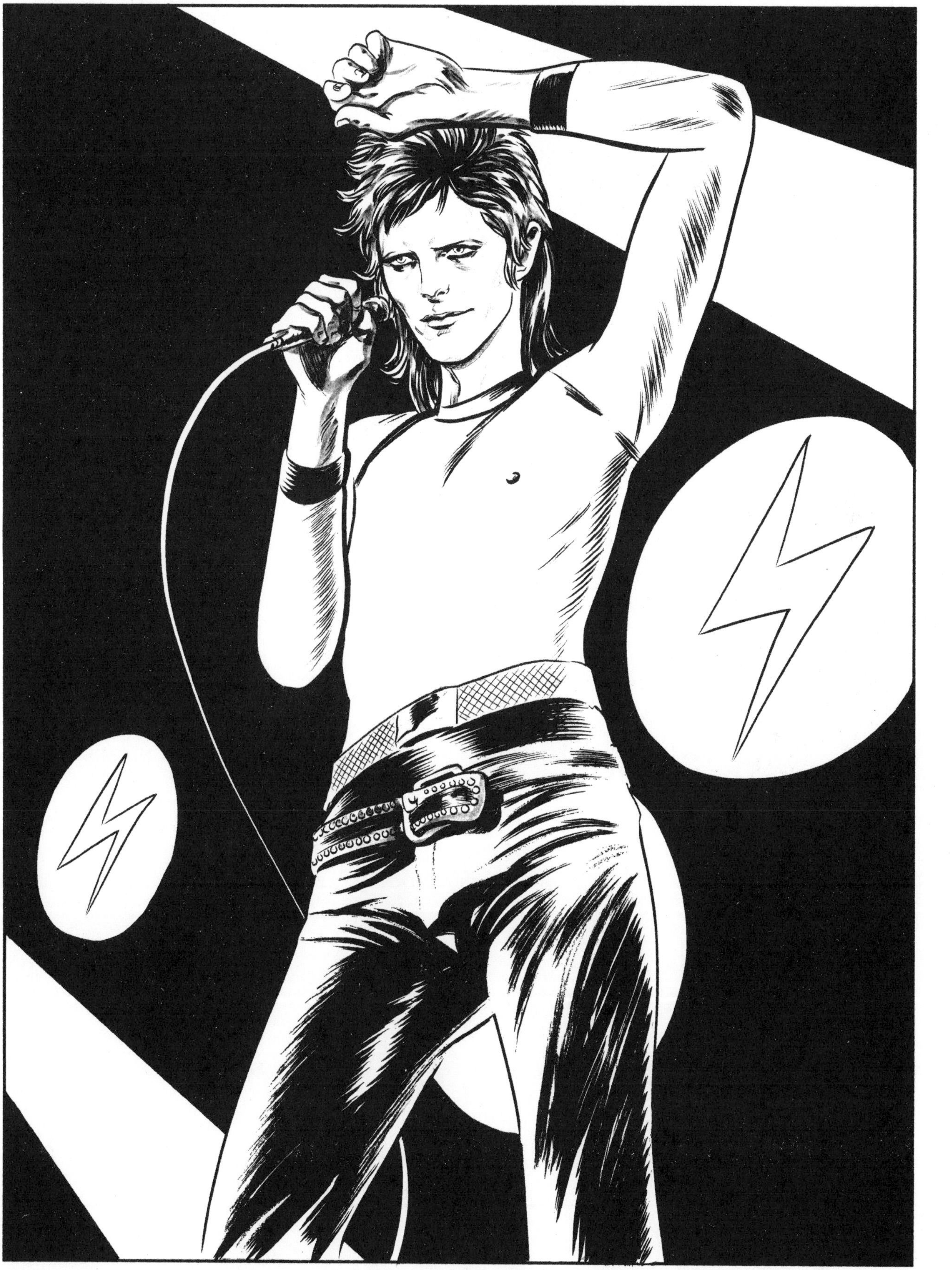

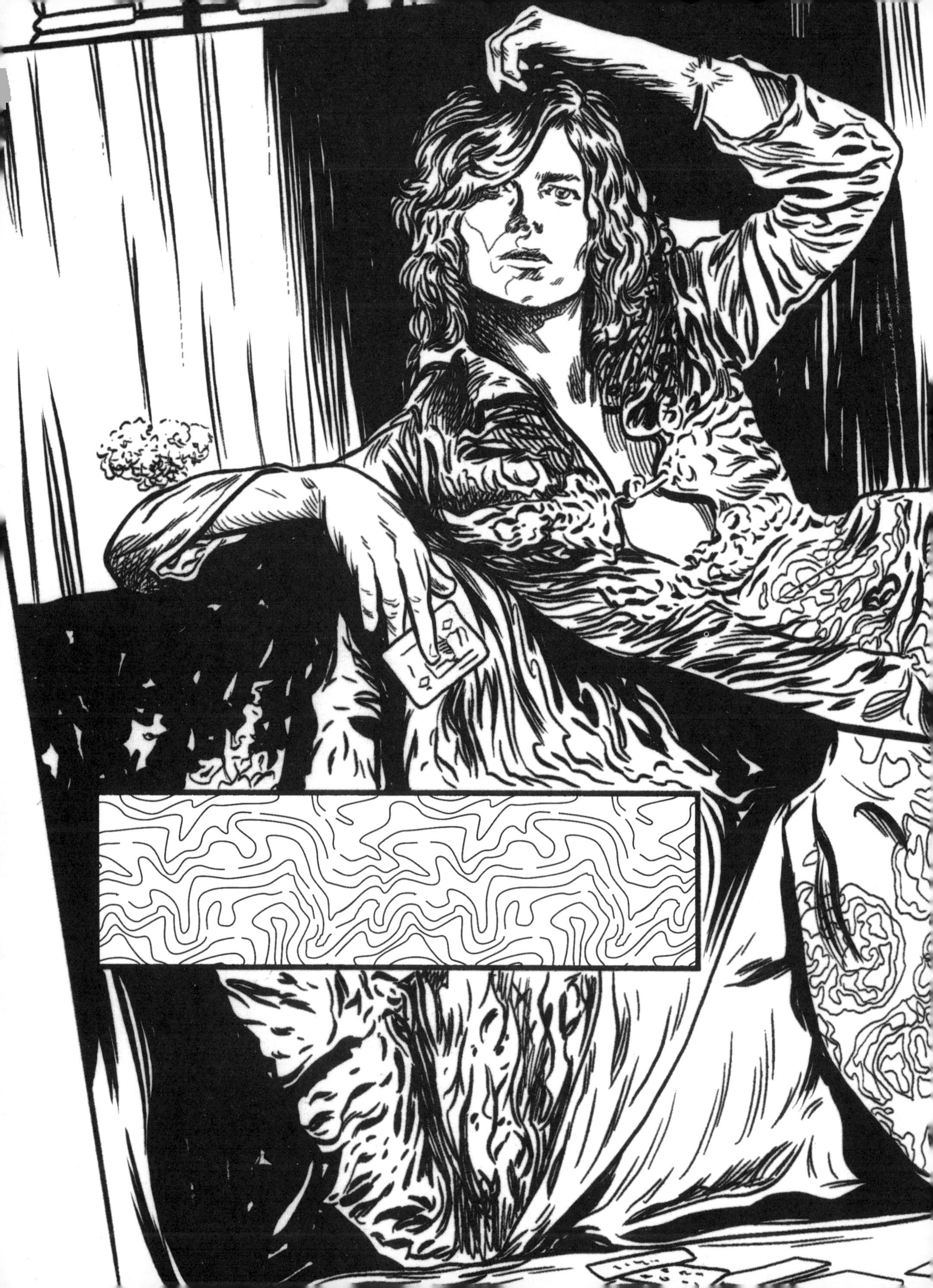

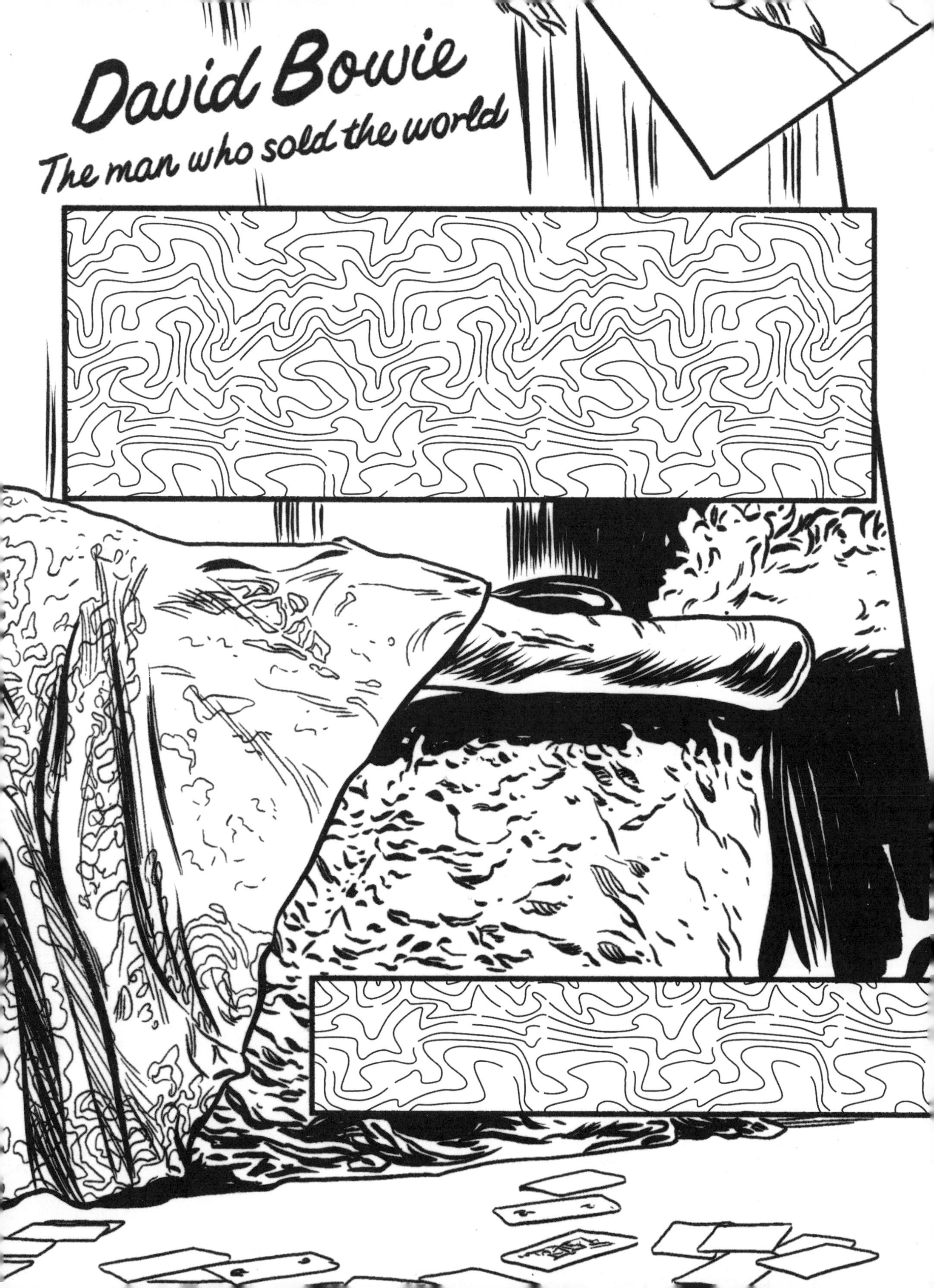
David Bowie
The man who sold the world

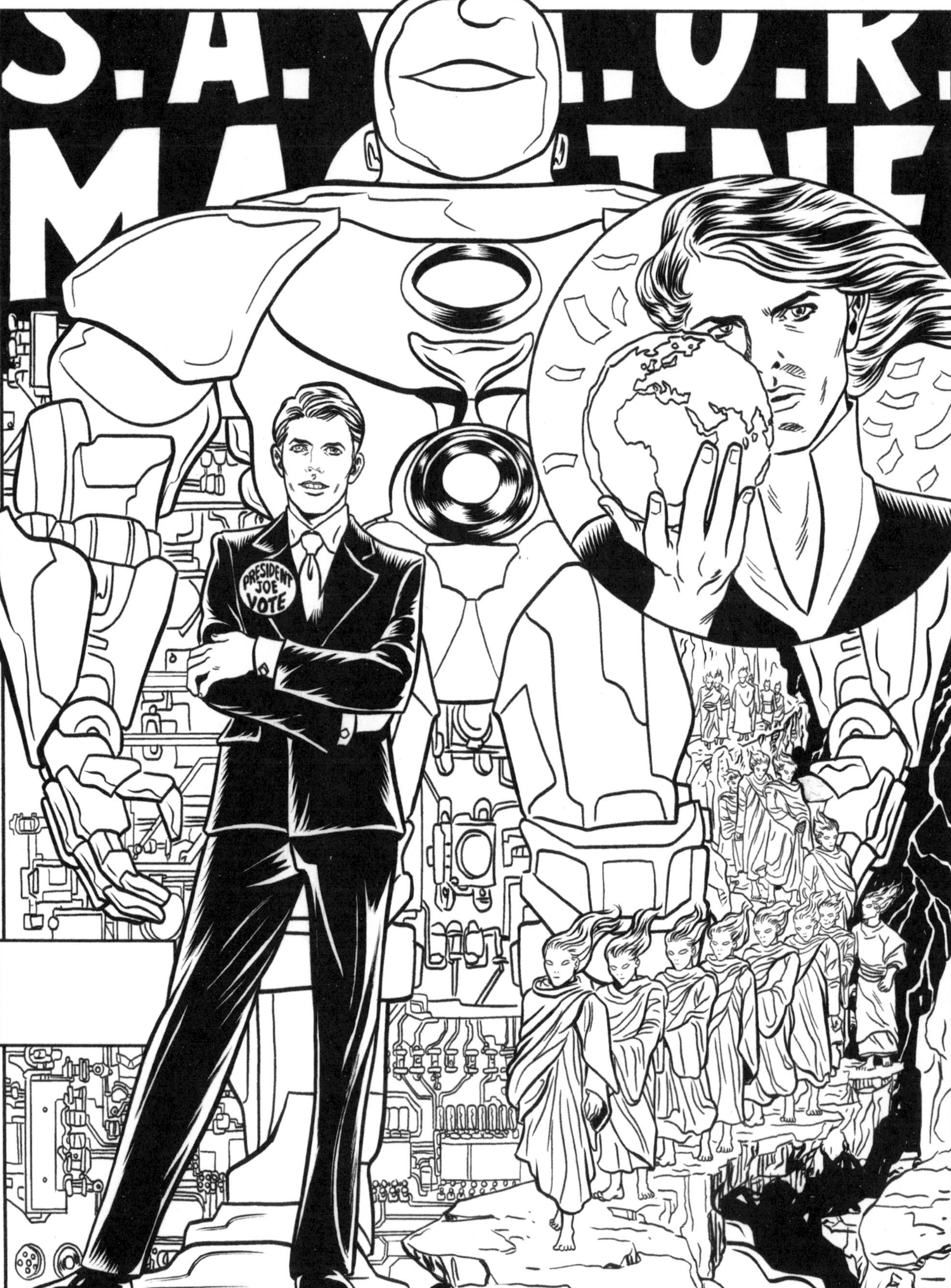
PRESIDENT JOE VOTE

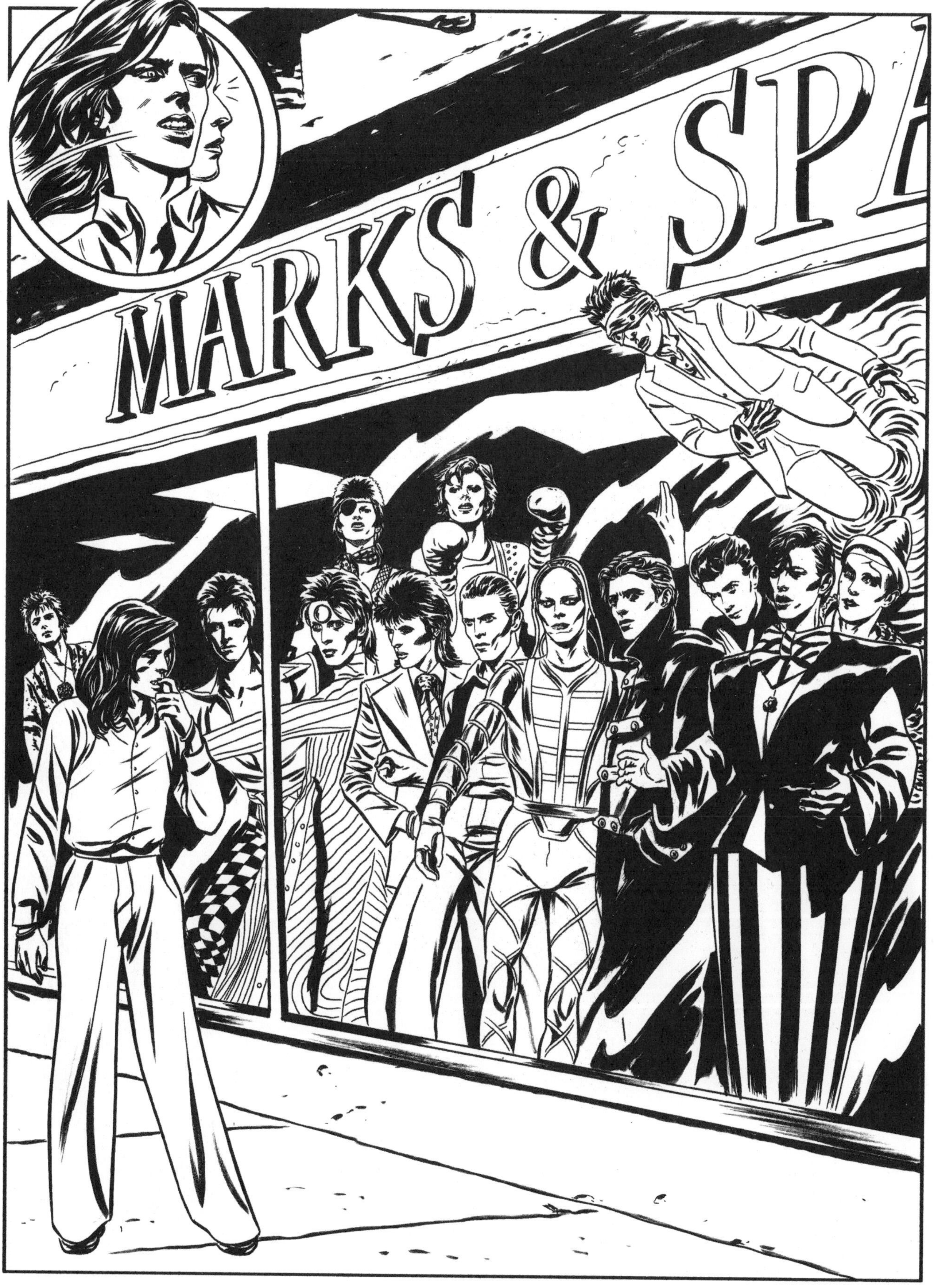
MARKS & SPA

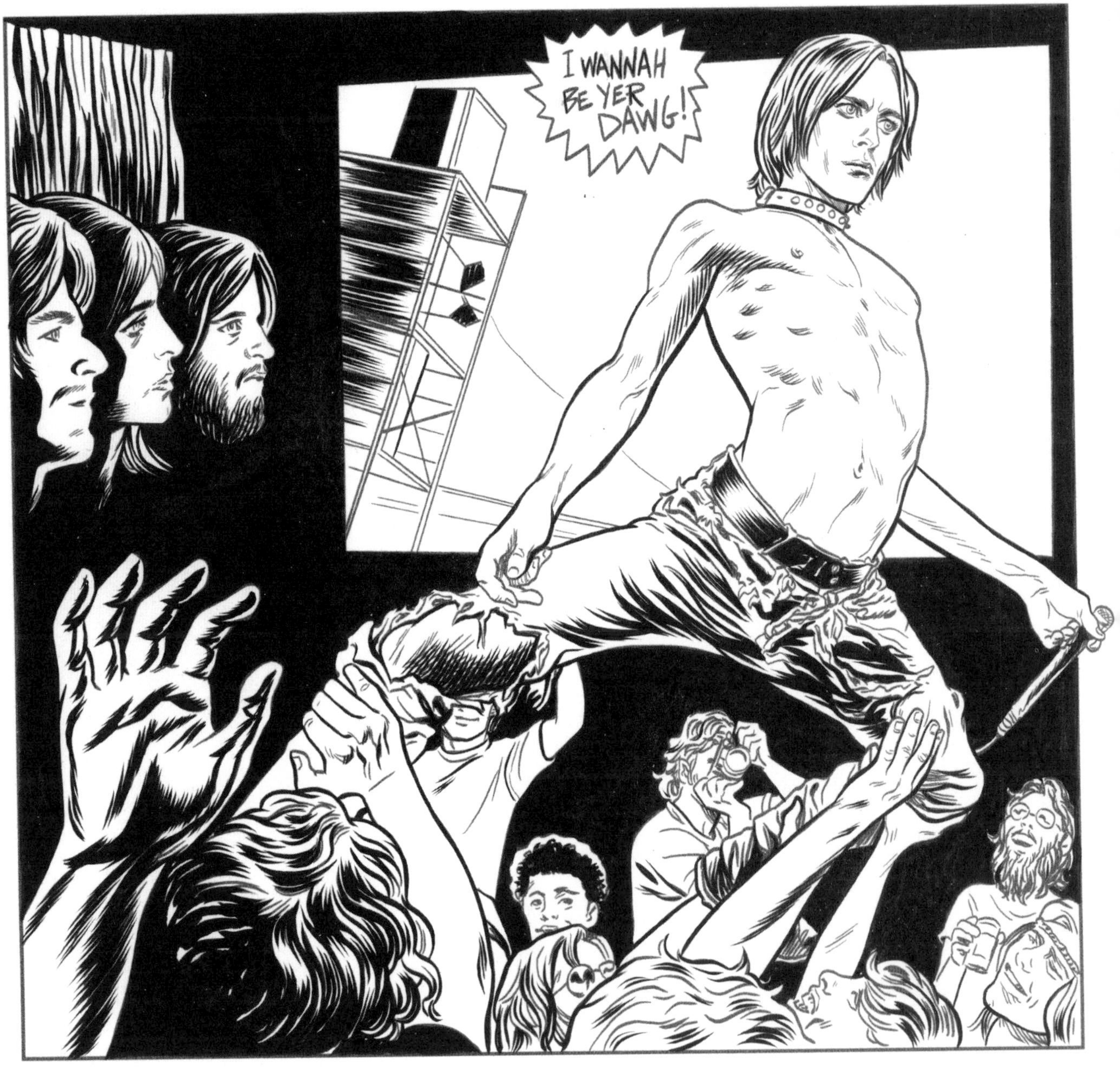
I WANNAH BE YER DAWG!

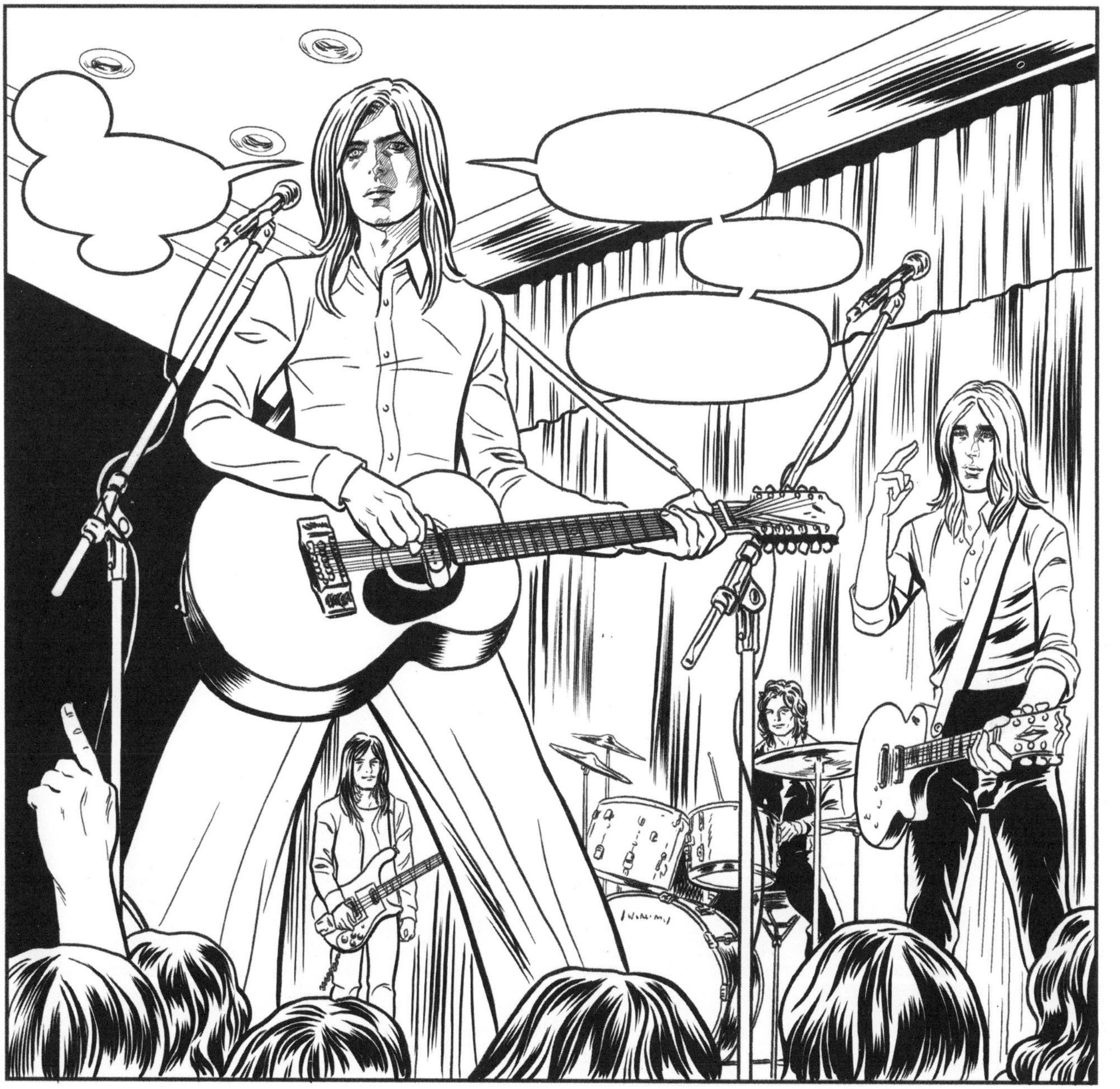

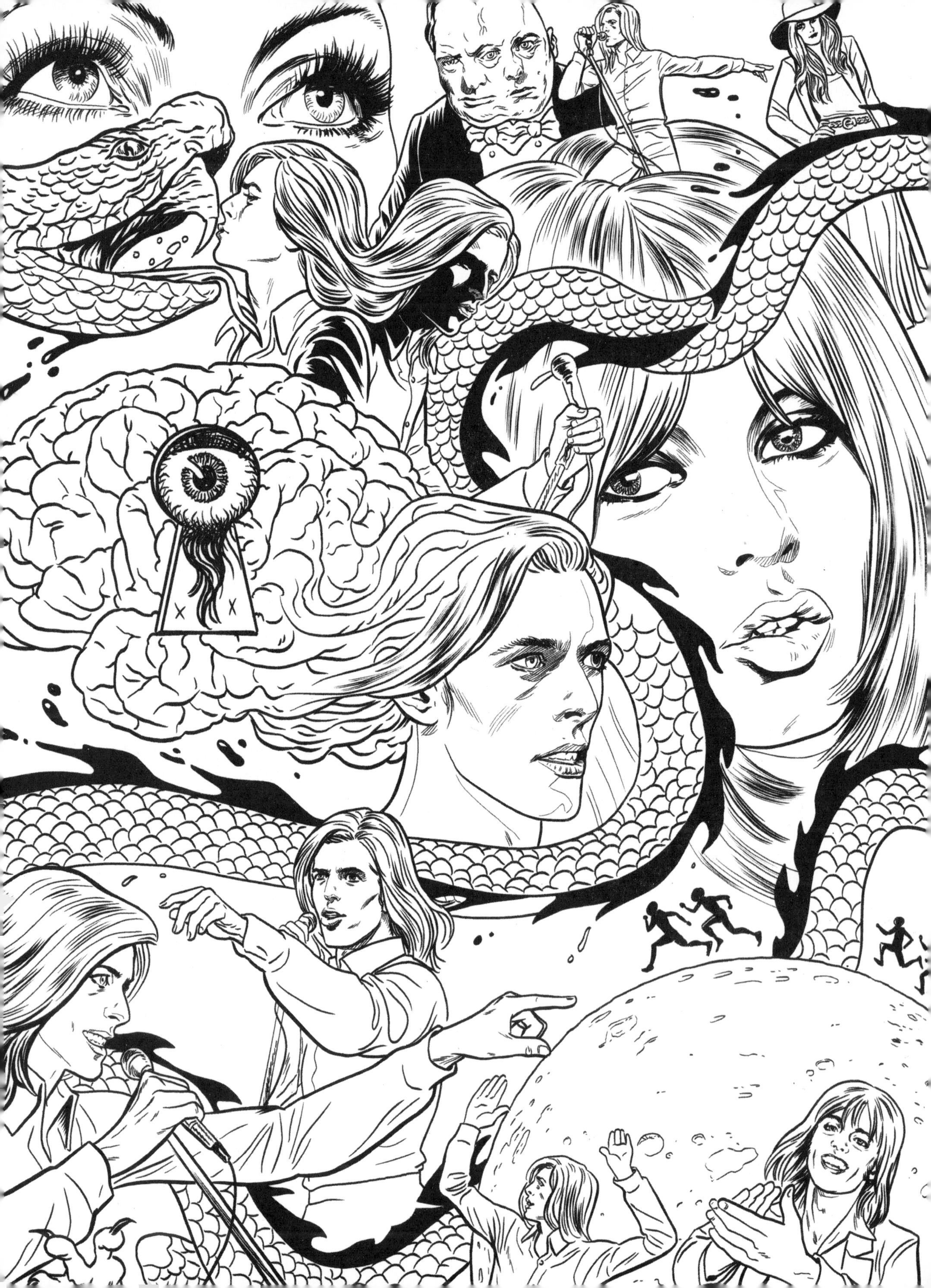

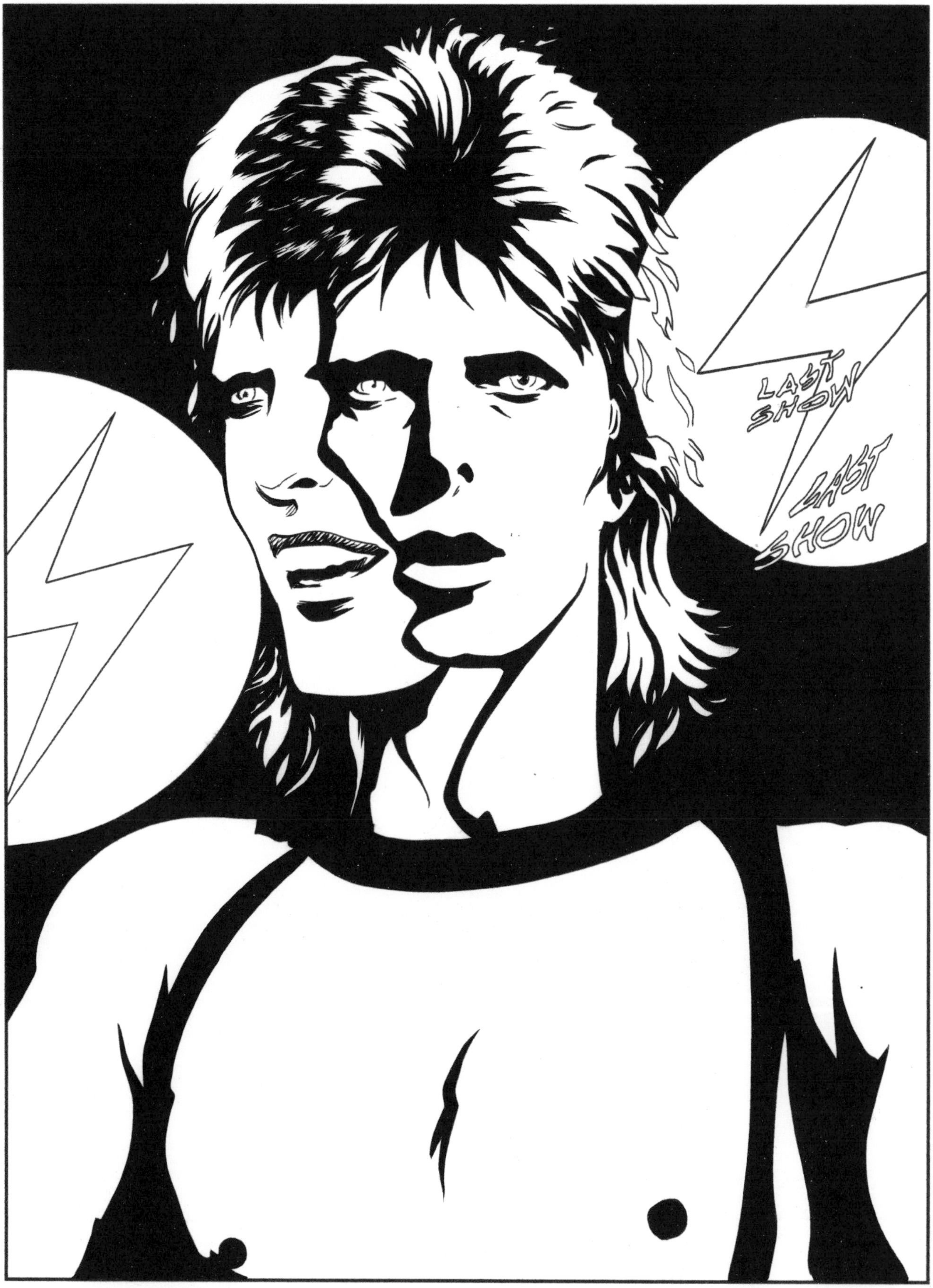
LAST SHOW
LAST SHOW

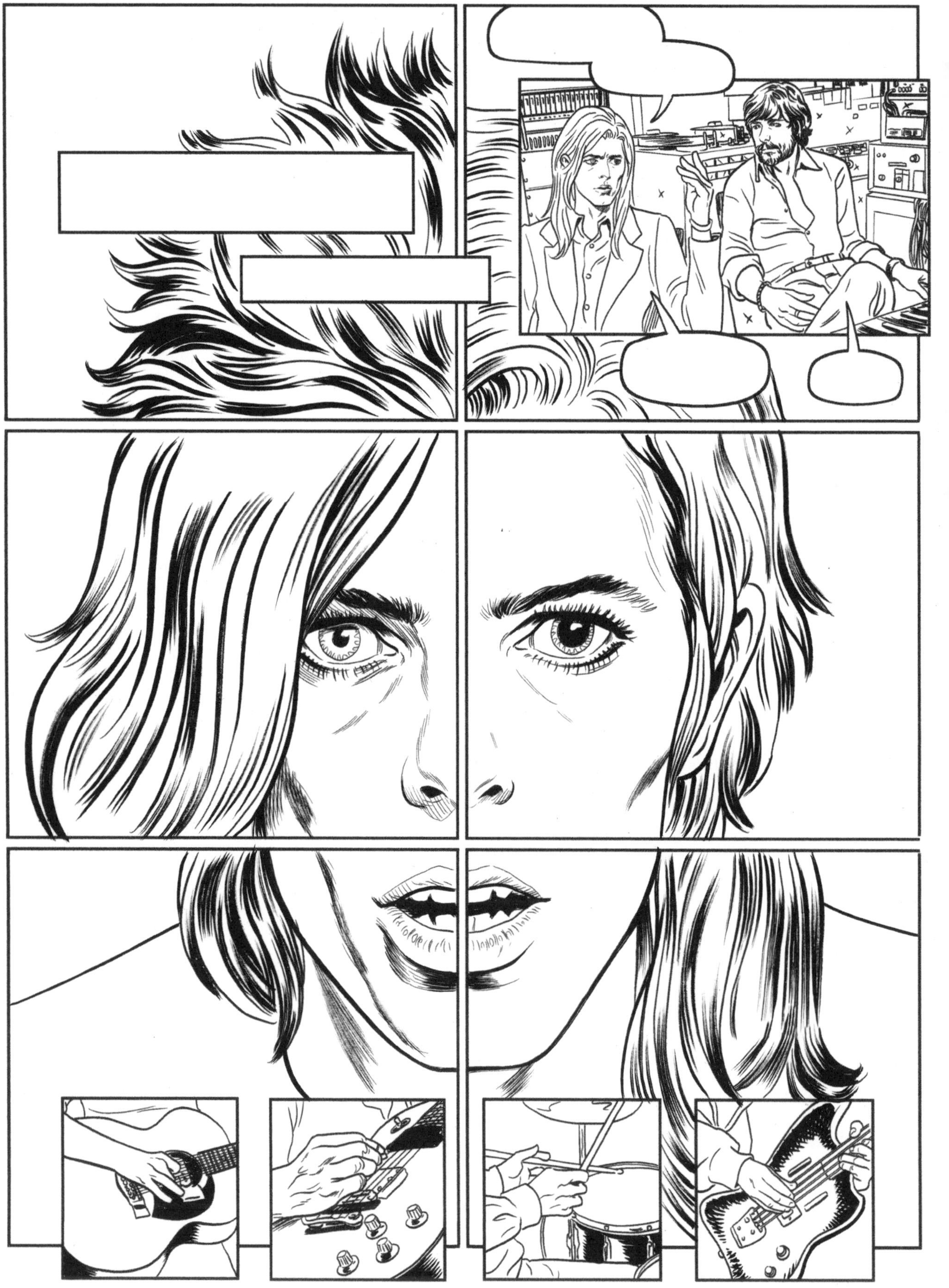

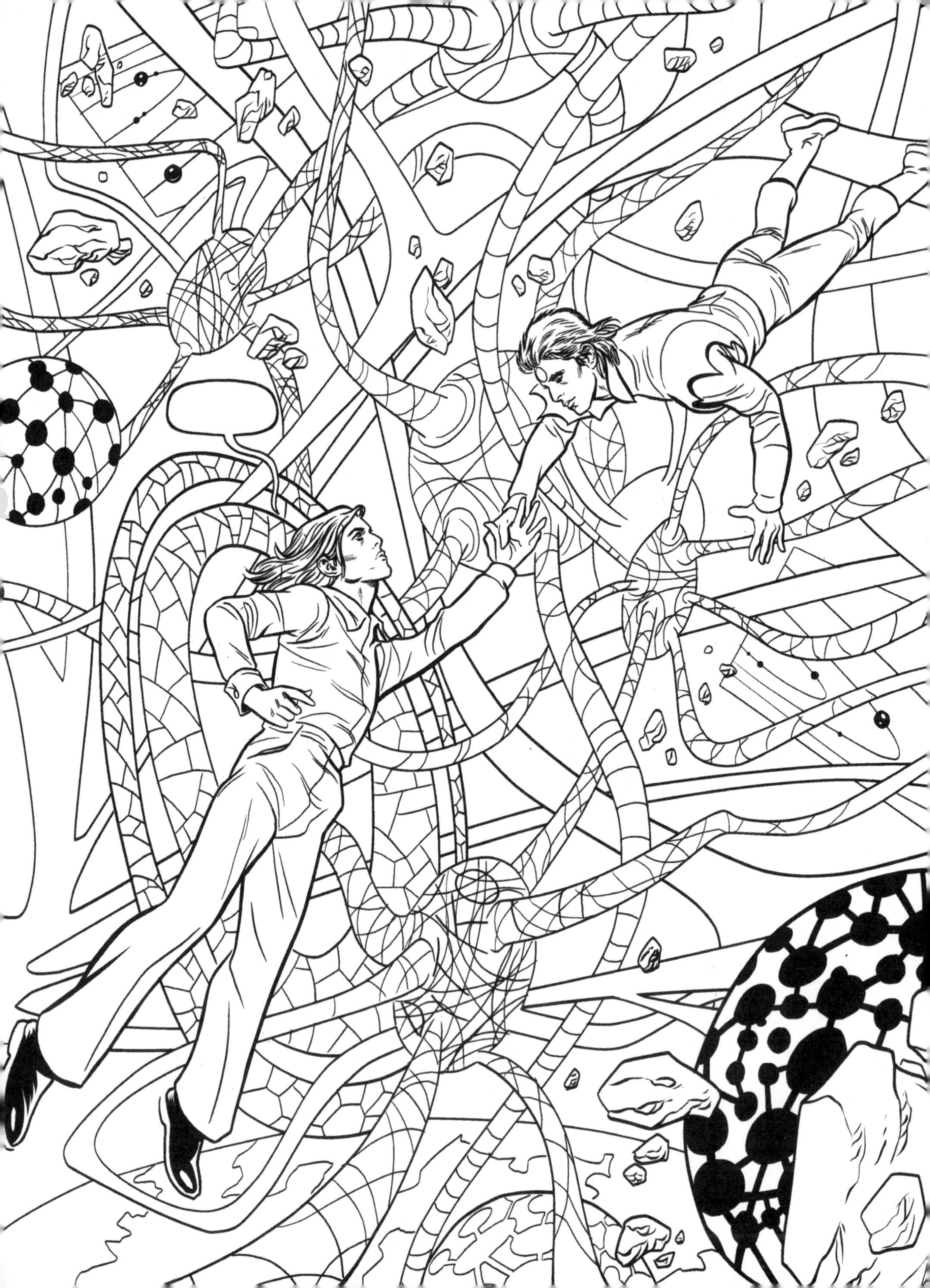

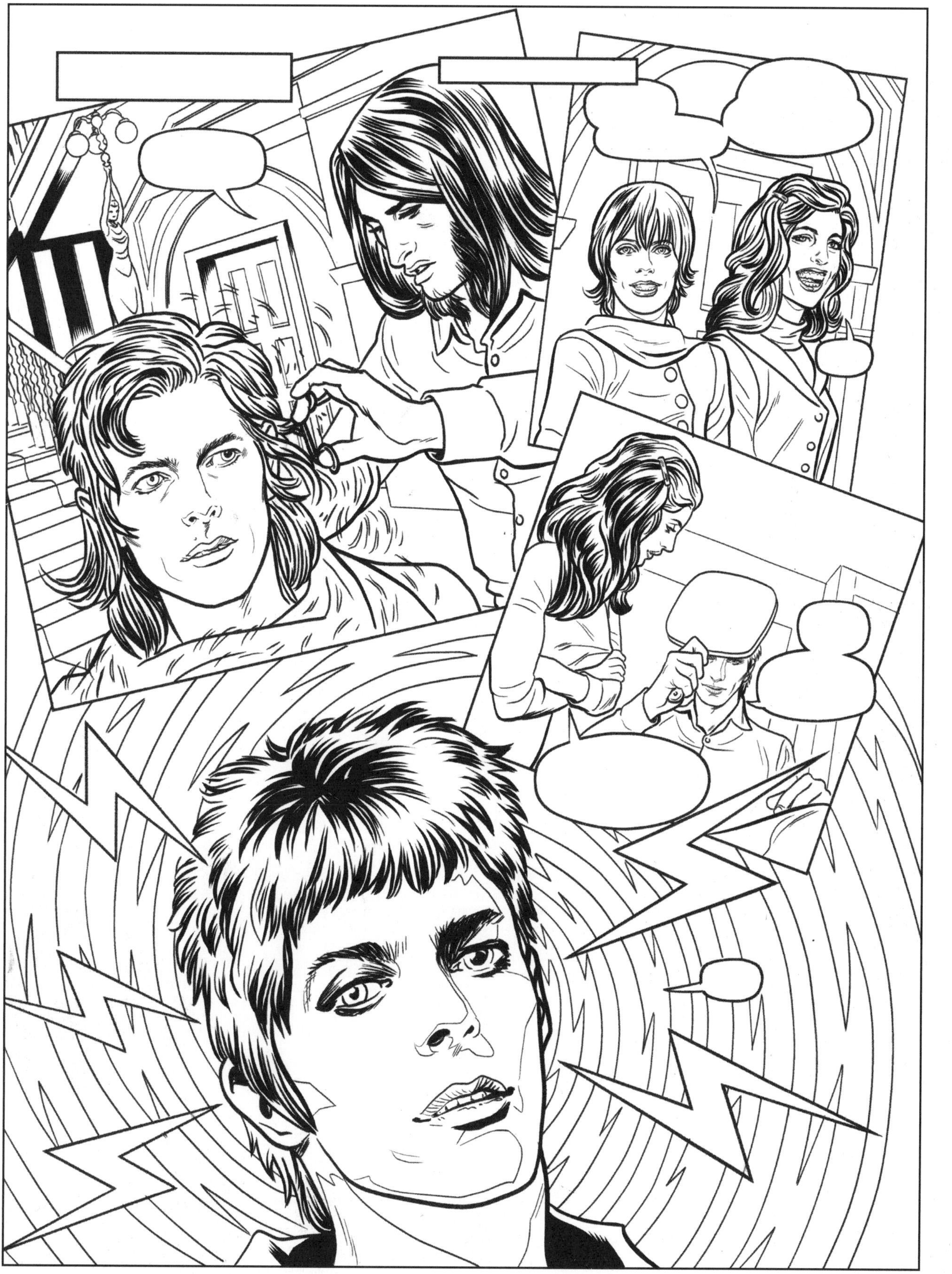

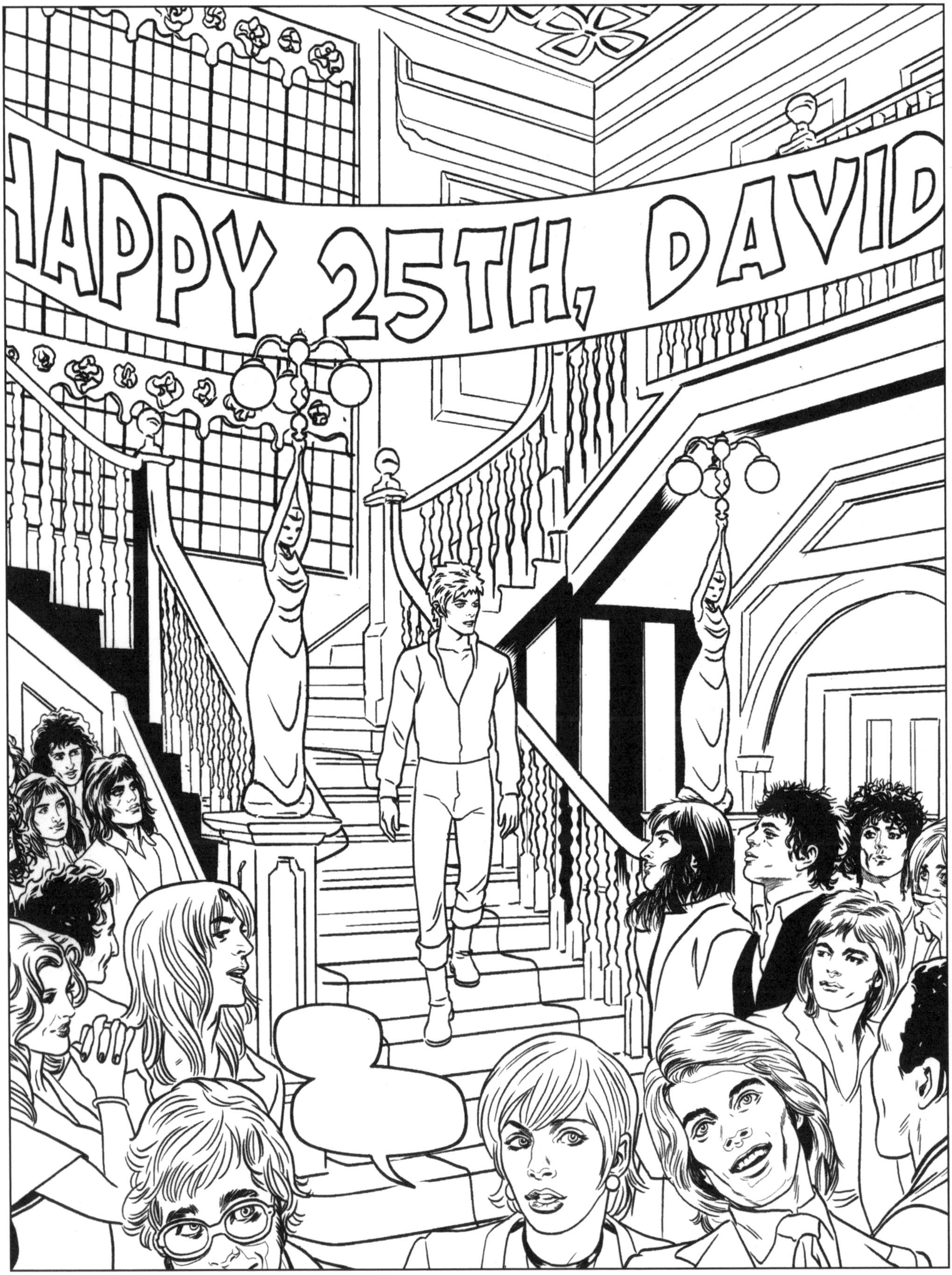
HAPPY 25TH, DAVID

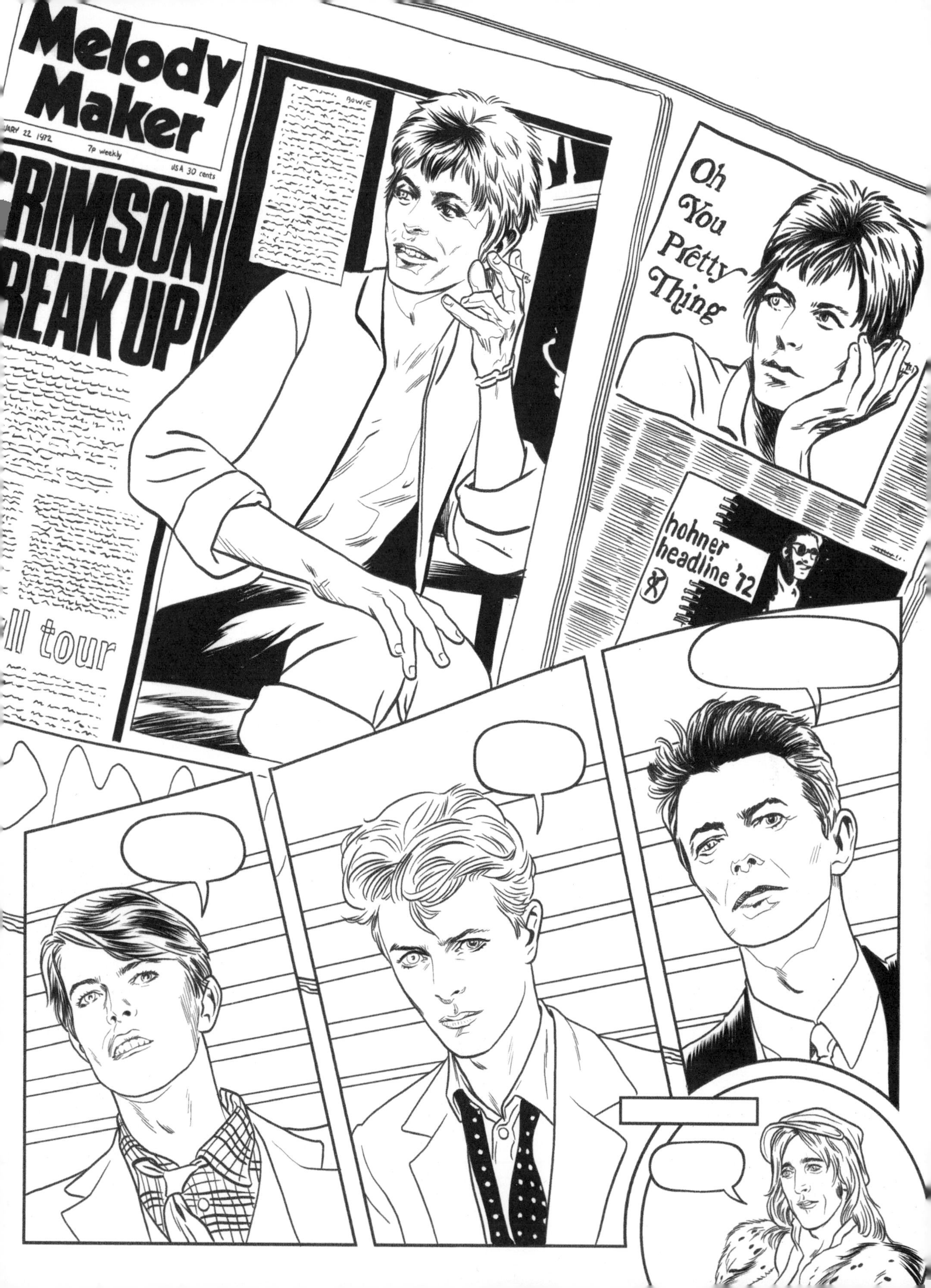
Melody Maker
UARY 22 1972
7p weekly
USA 30 cents
RIMSON
REAK UP
ll tour
BOWIE
Oh You Pretty Thing
hohner headline '72

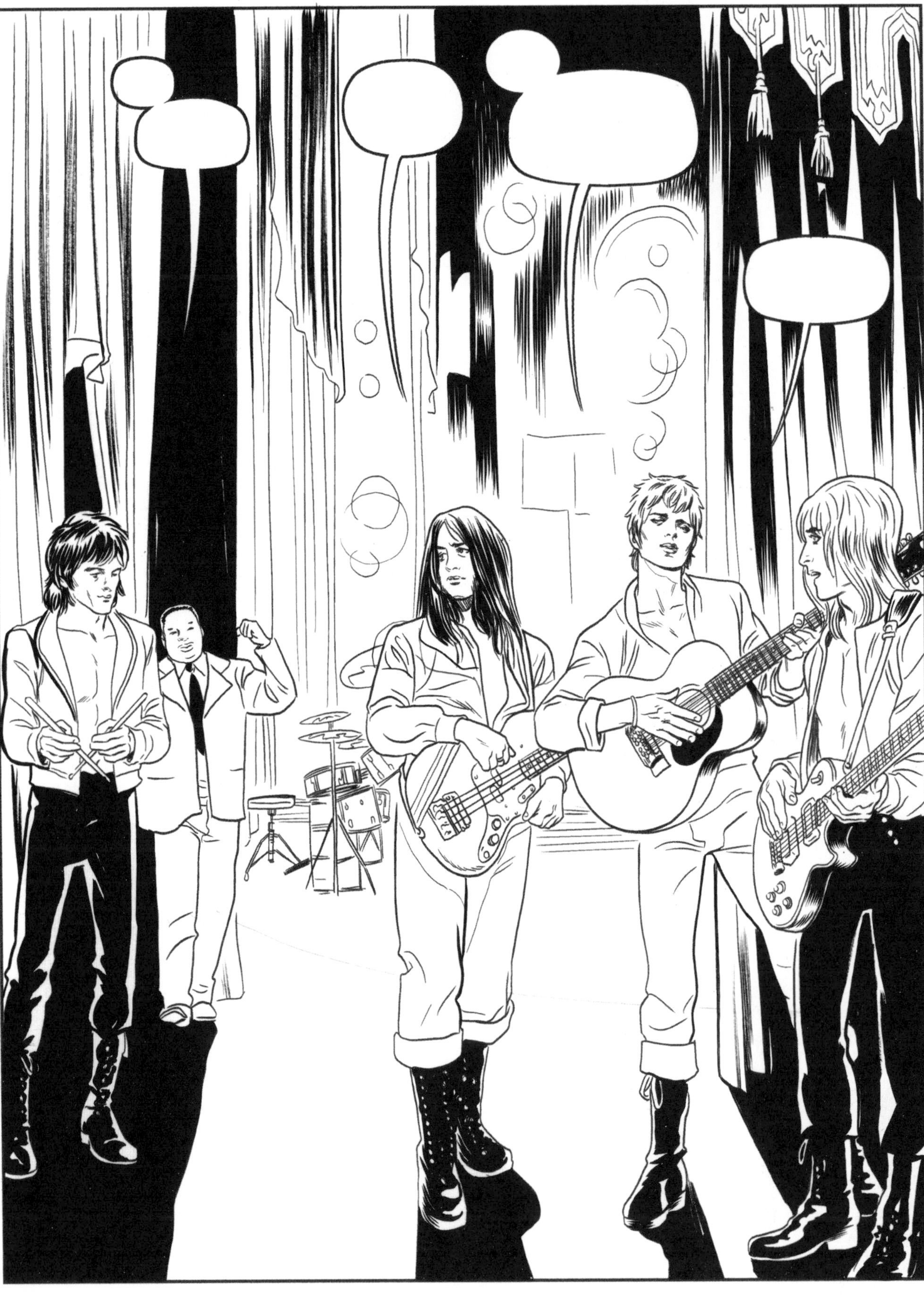

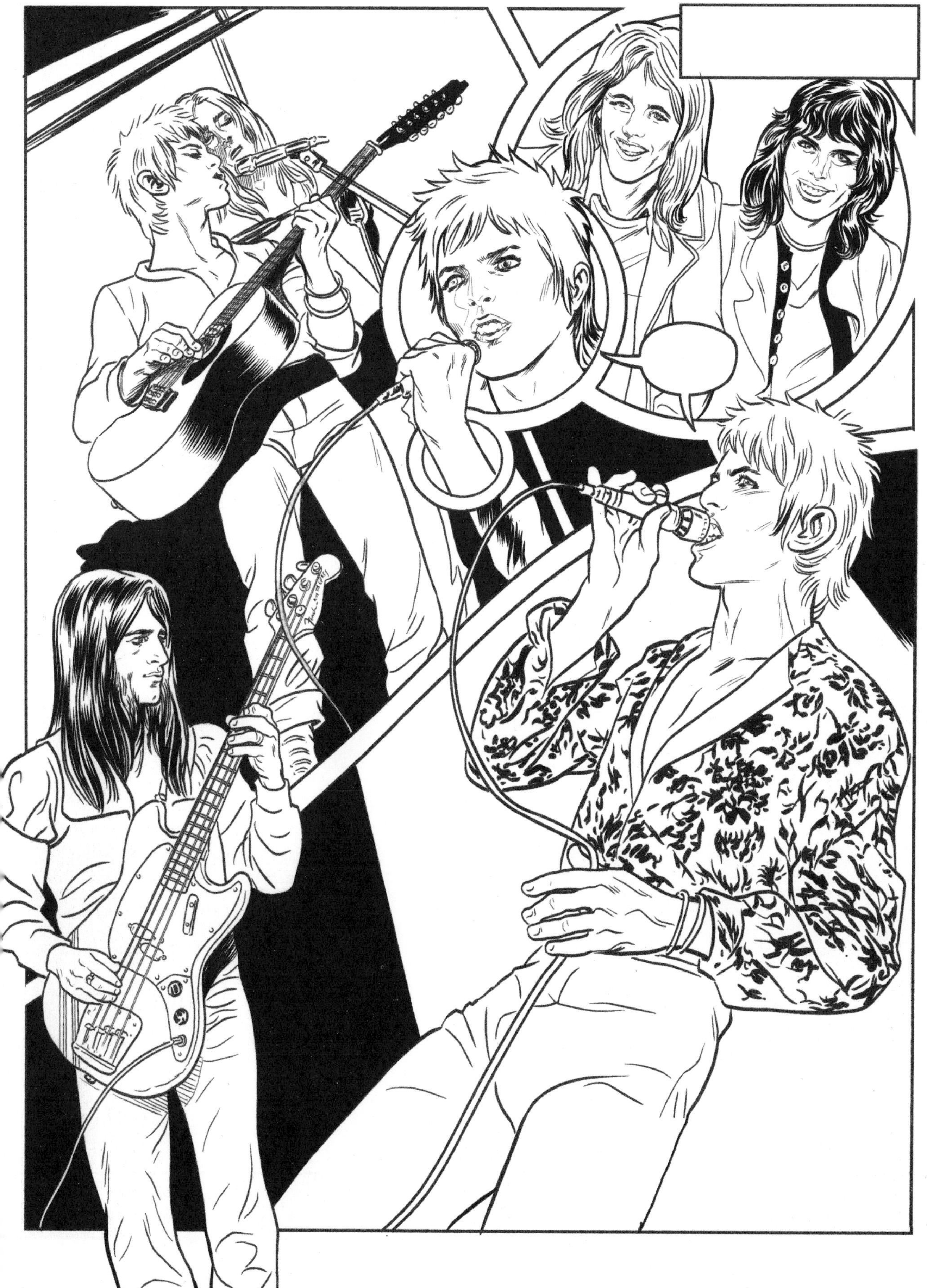

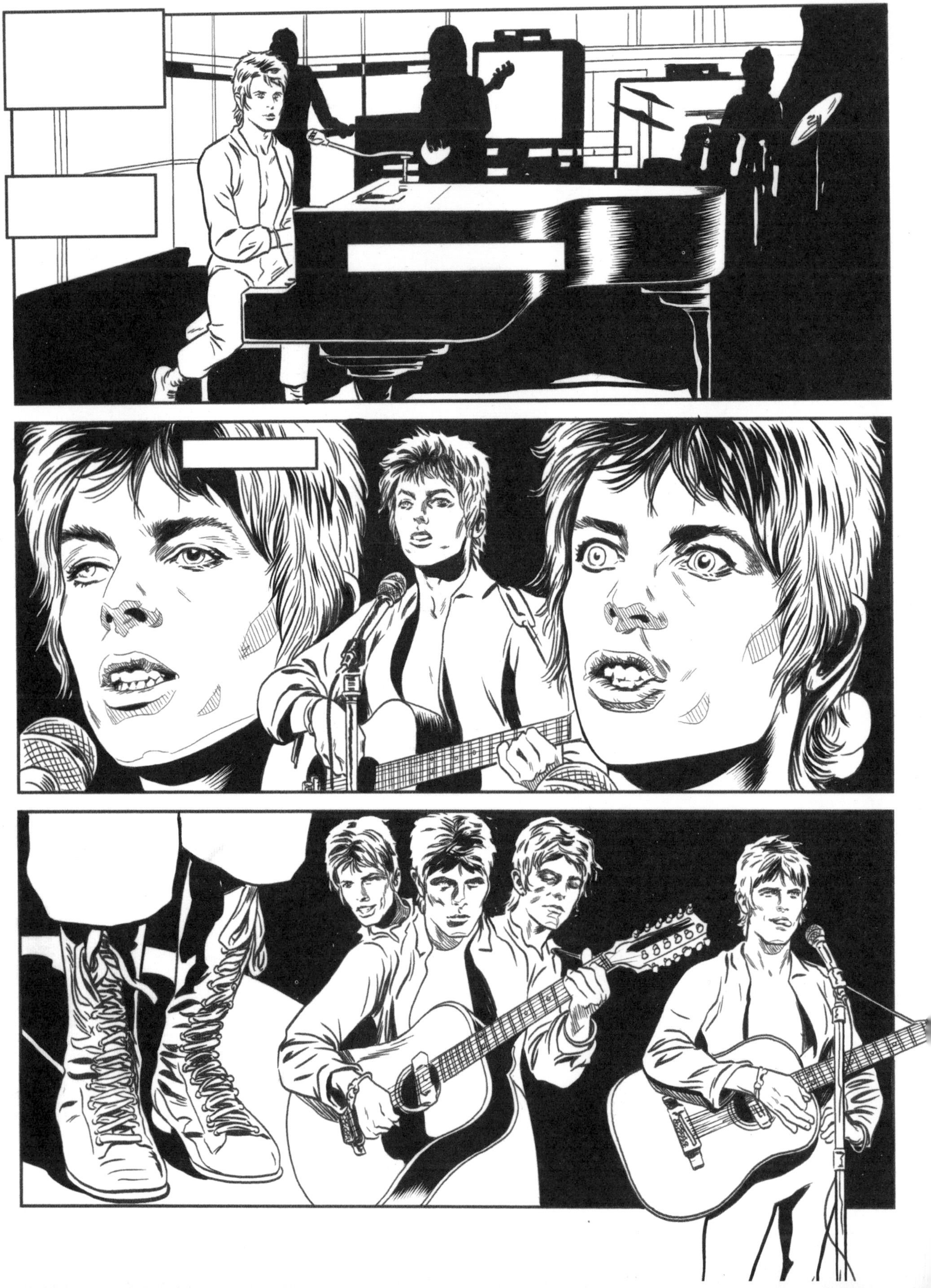

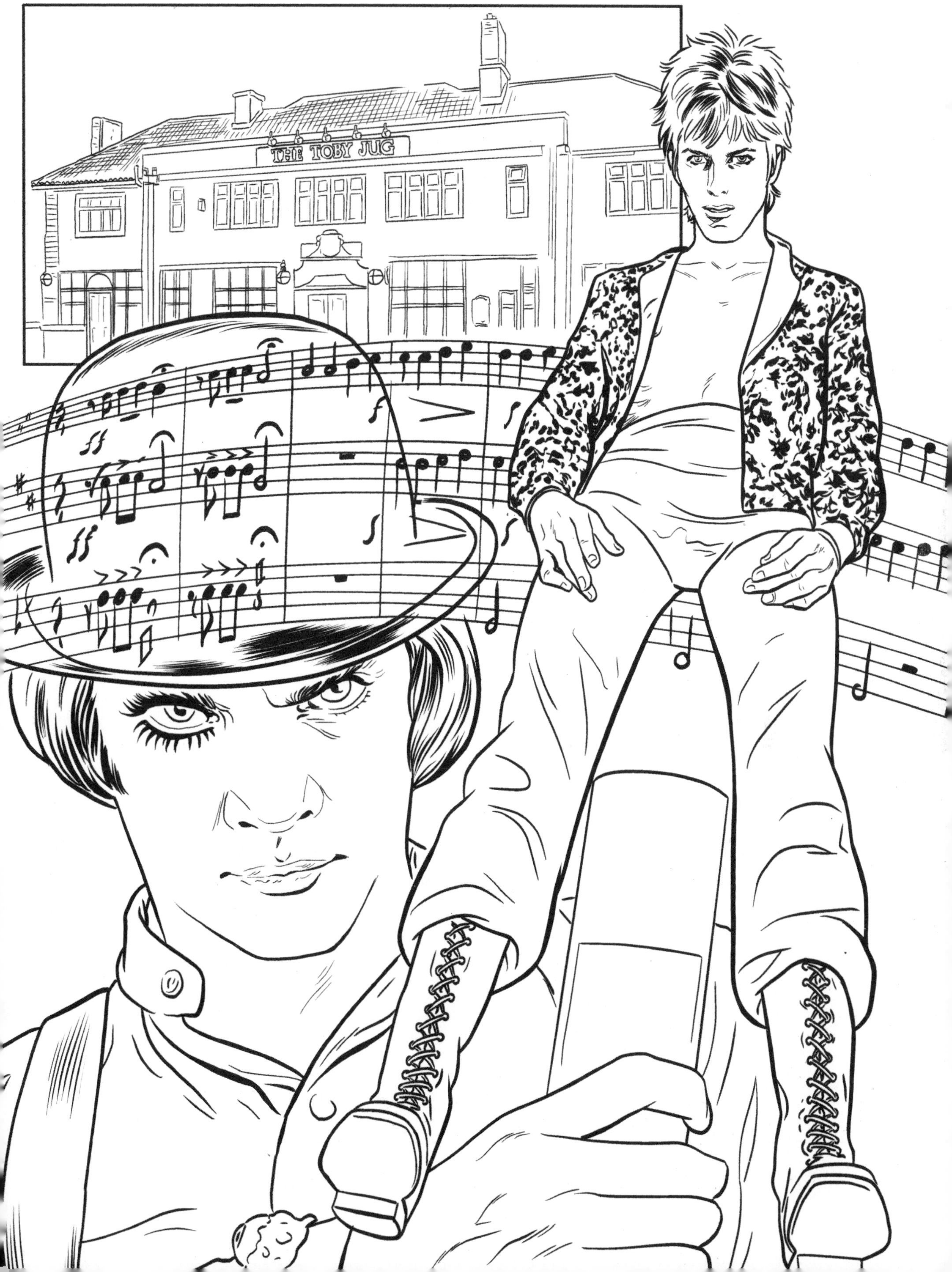
THE TOBY JUG

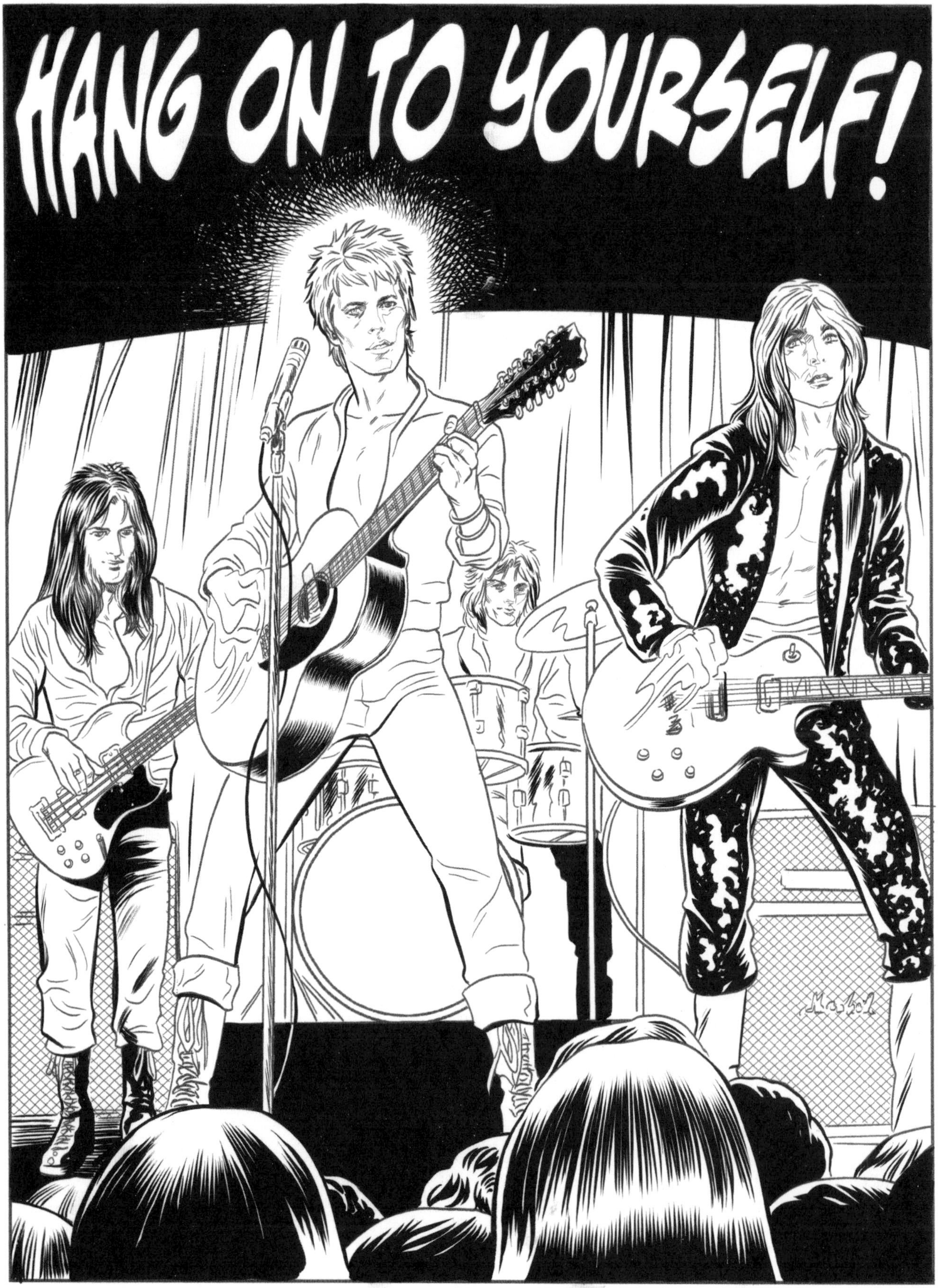
HANG ON TO YOURSELF!

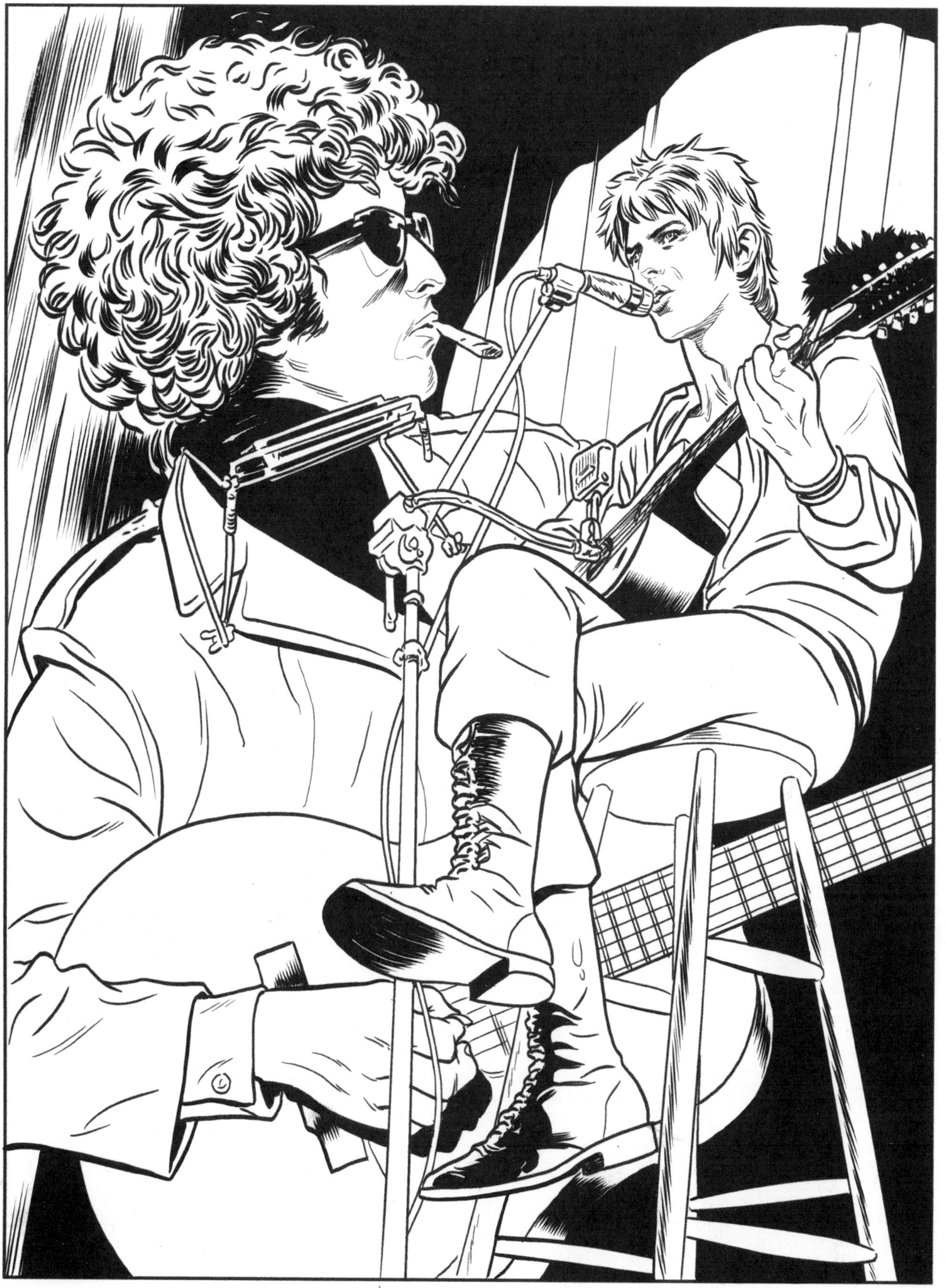

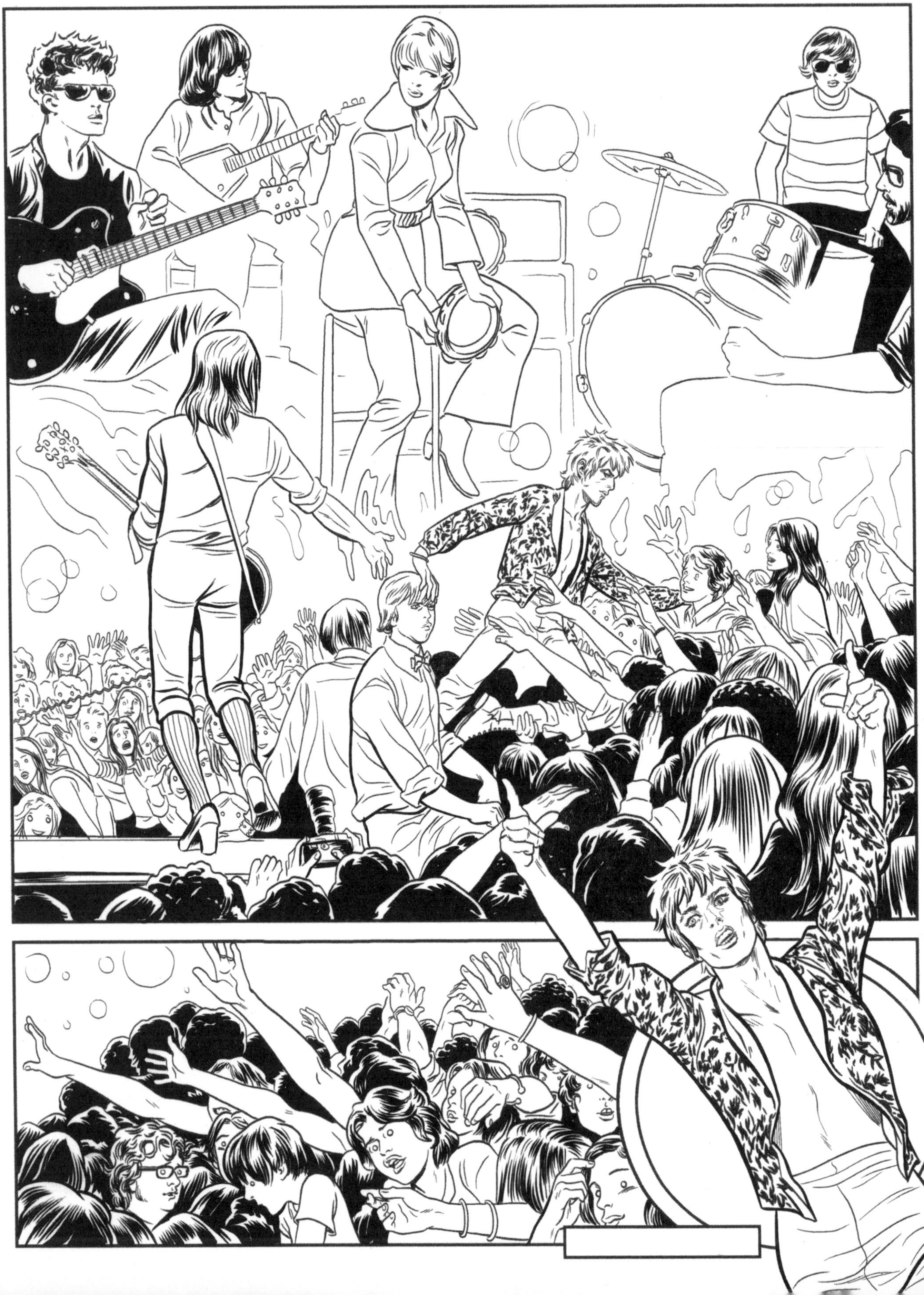

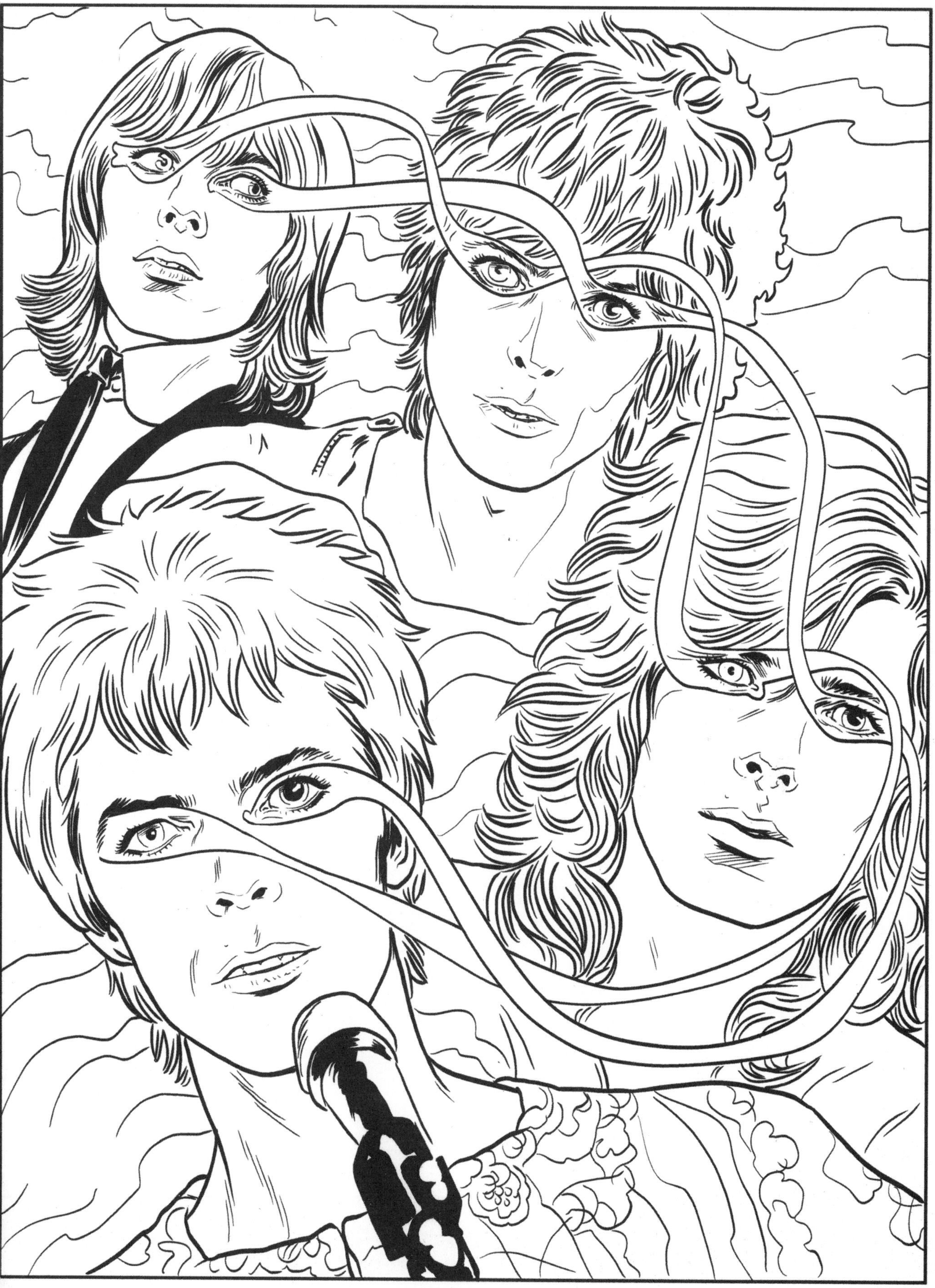

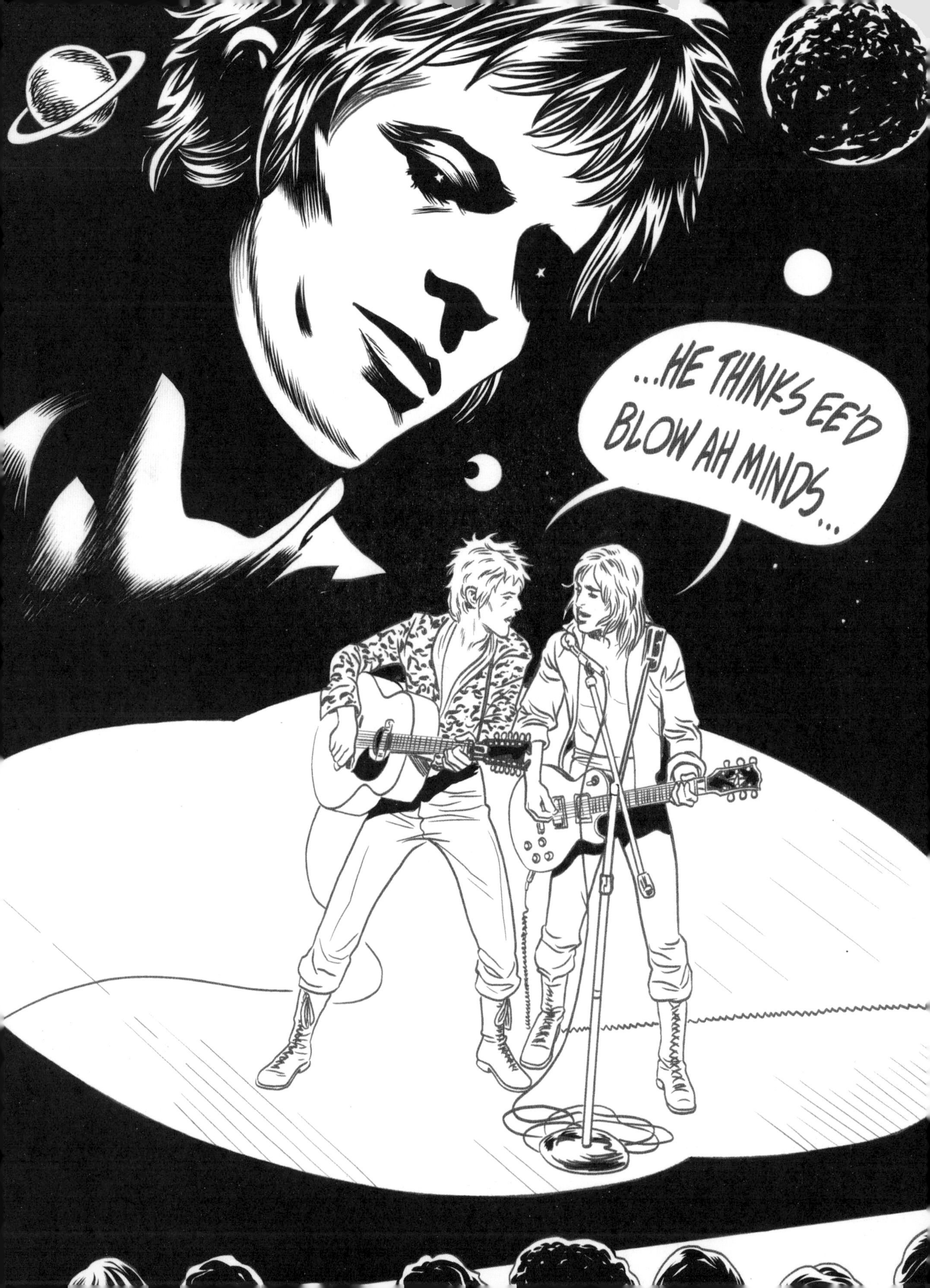
...HE THINKS EE'D BLOW AH MINDS...

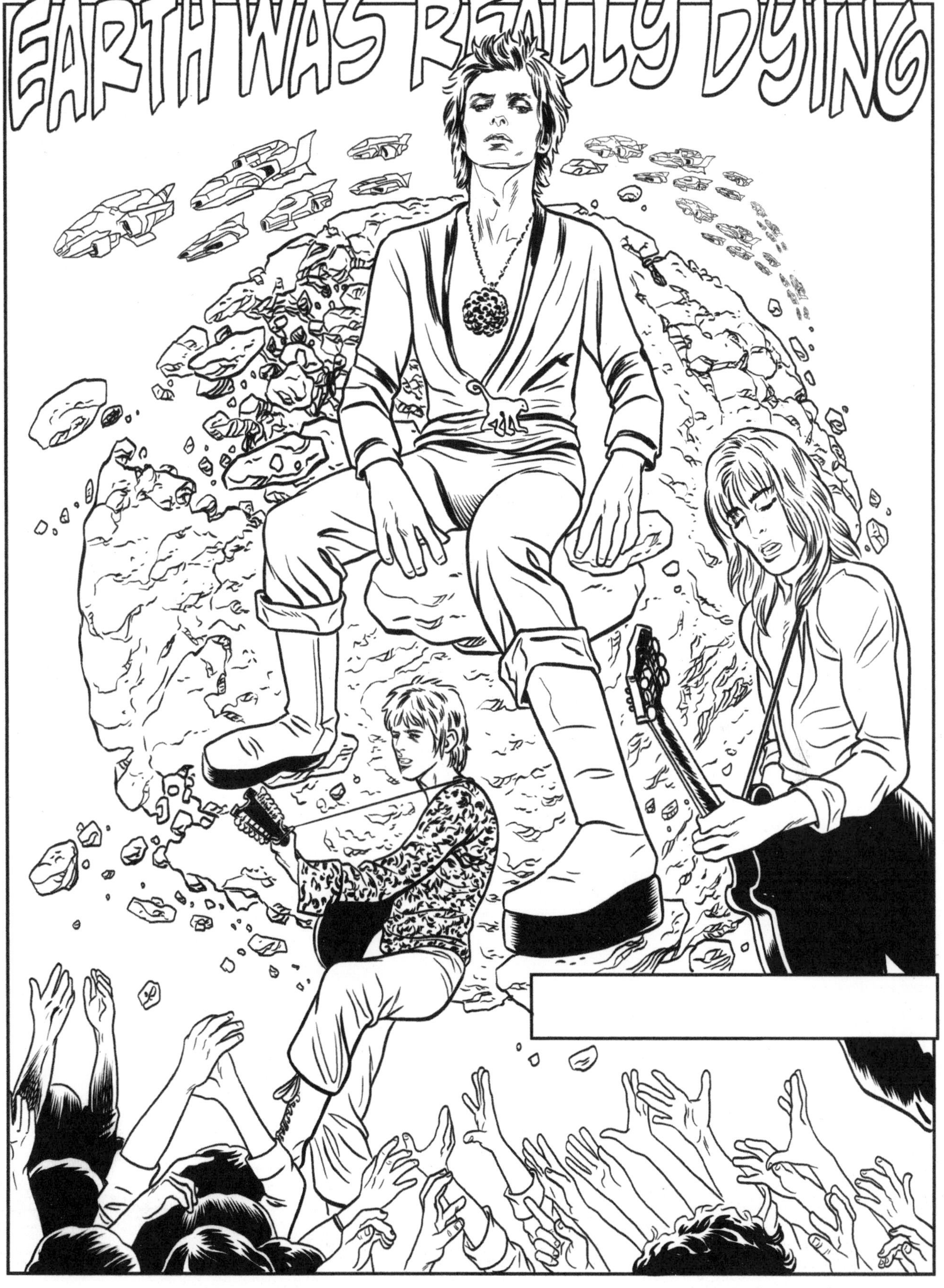
EARTH WAS REALLY DYING

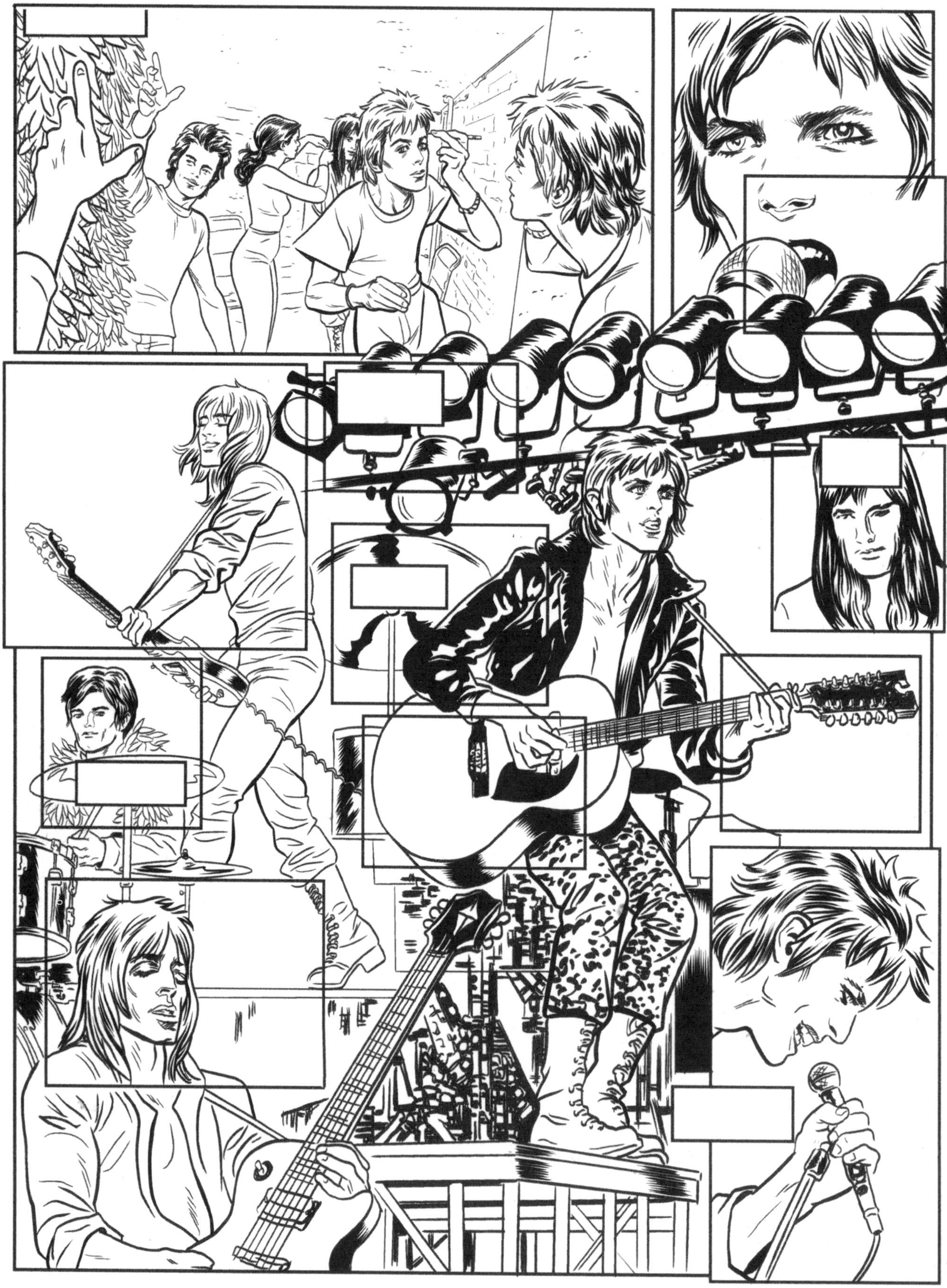

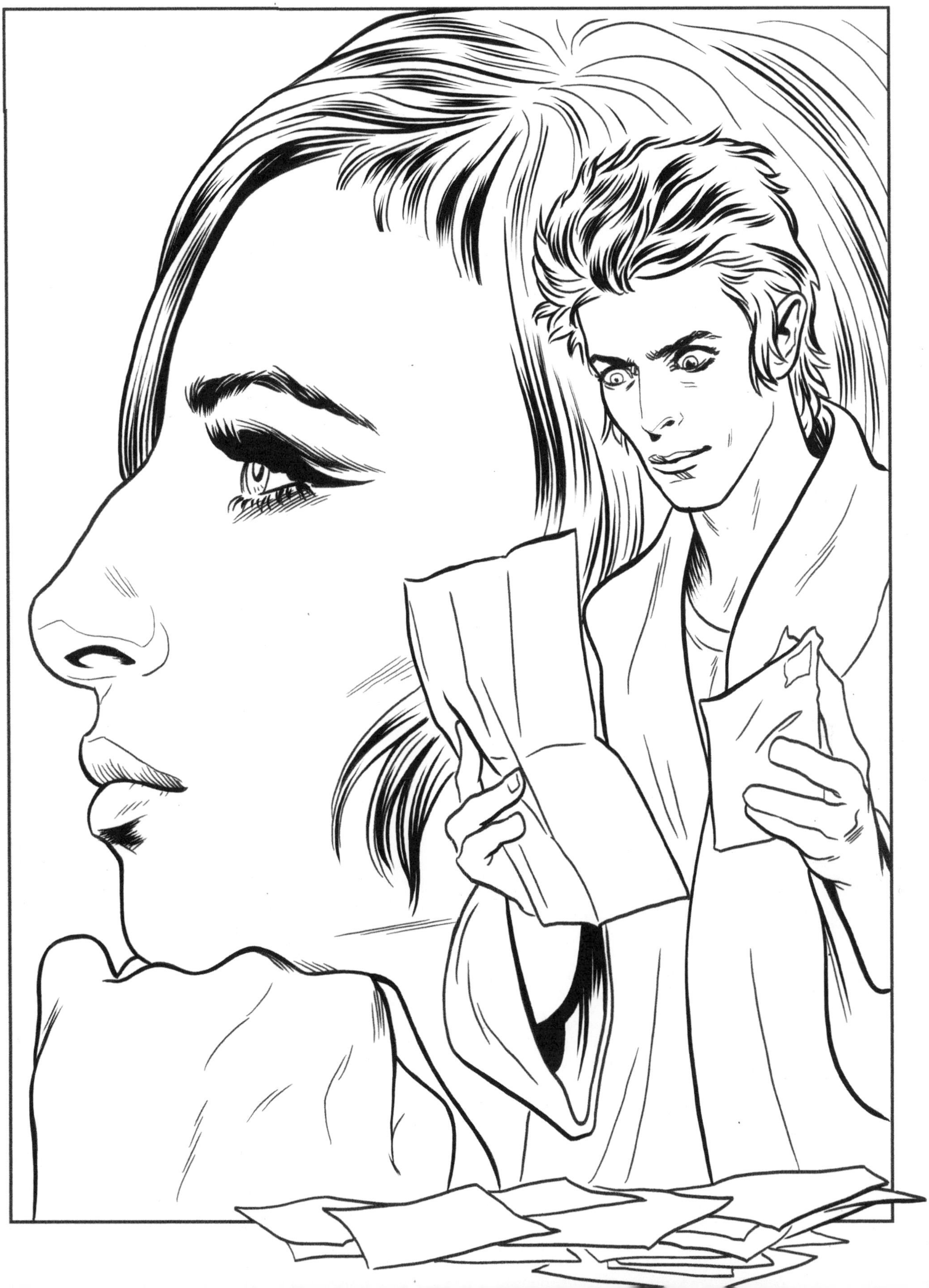

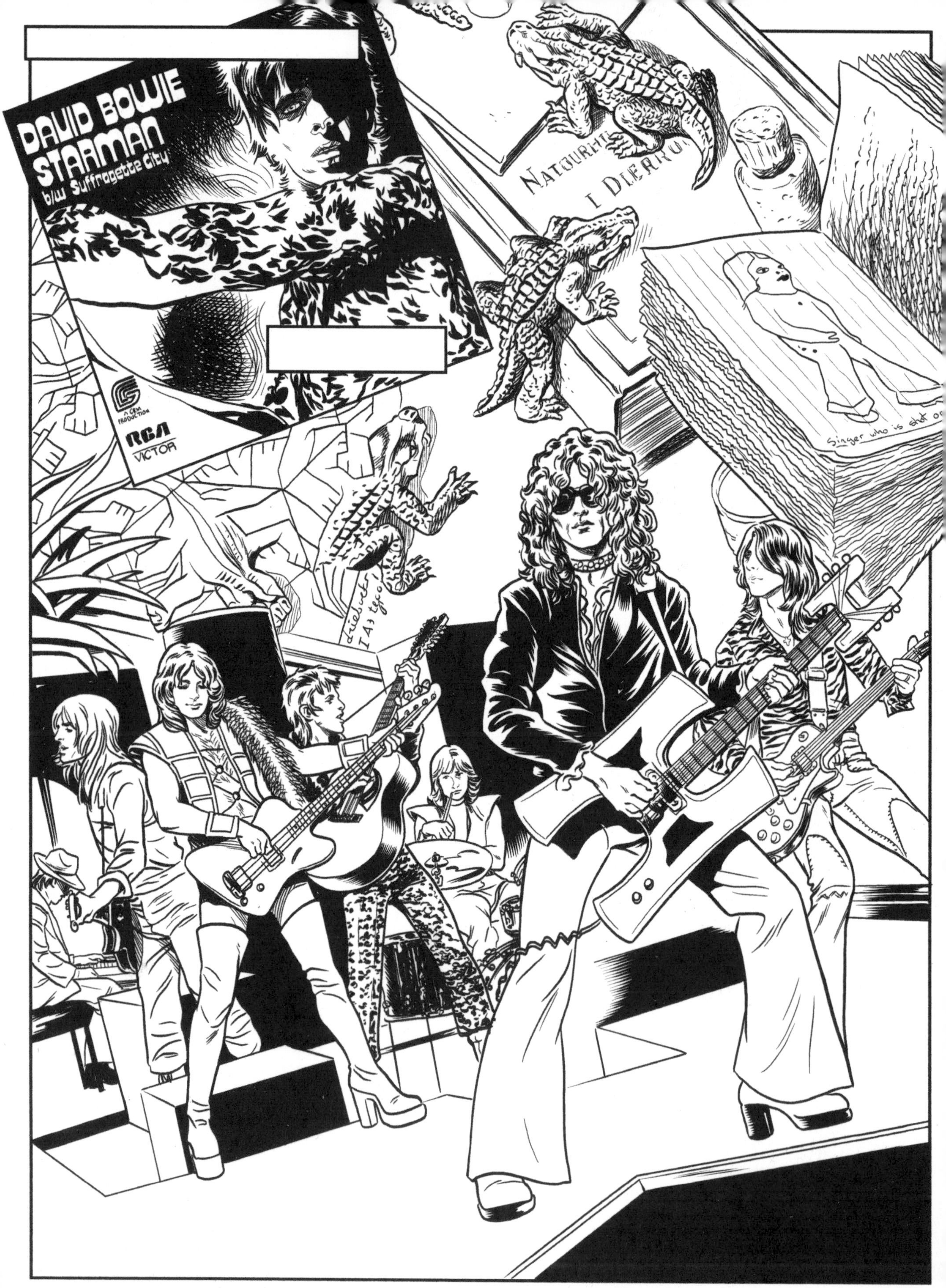
DAVID BOWIE
STARMAN
b/w Suffragette City
A GEM PRODUCTION
RCA
VICTOR

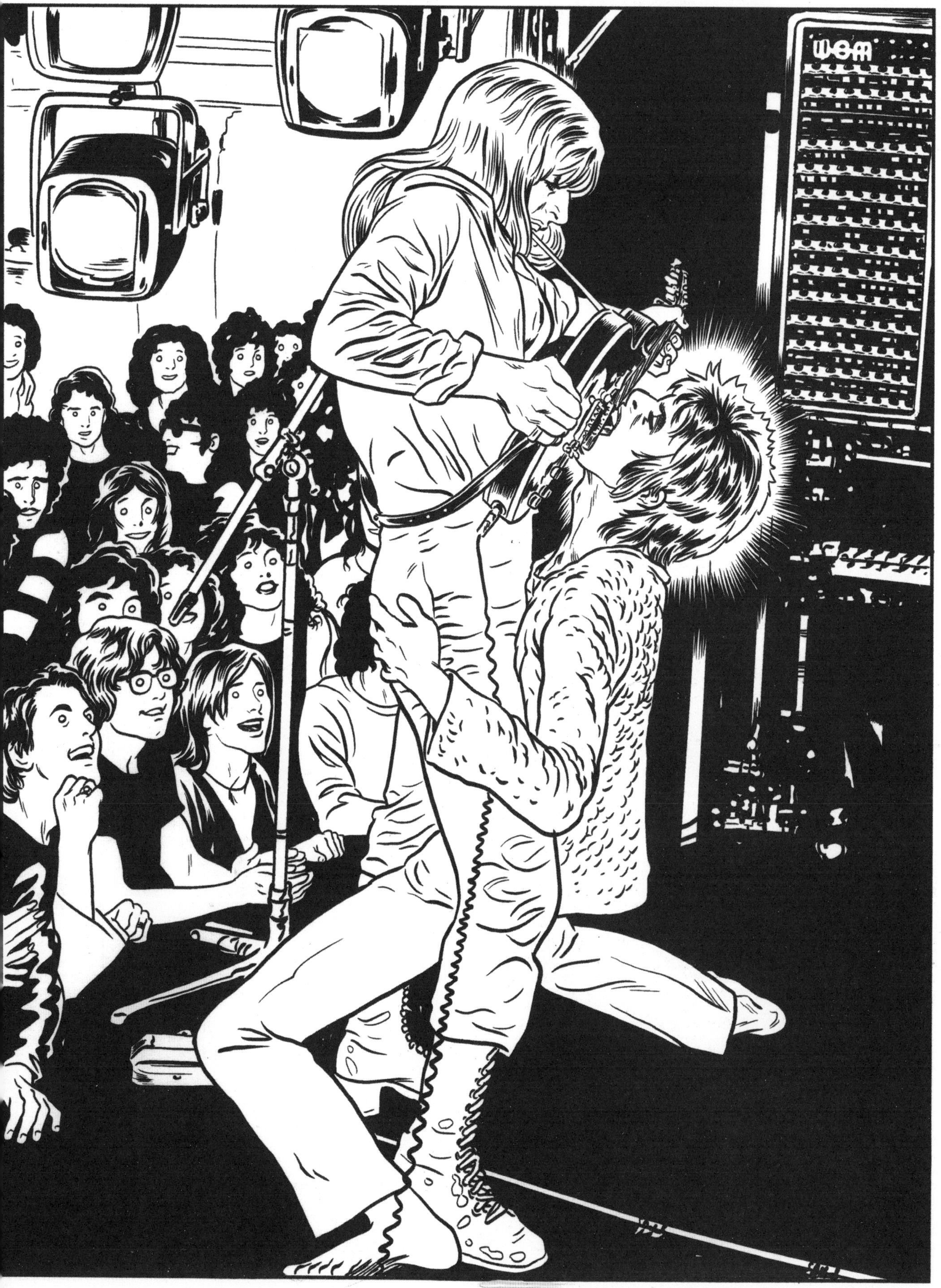
WEM

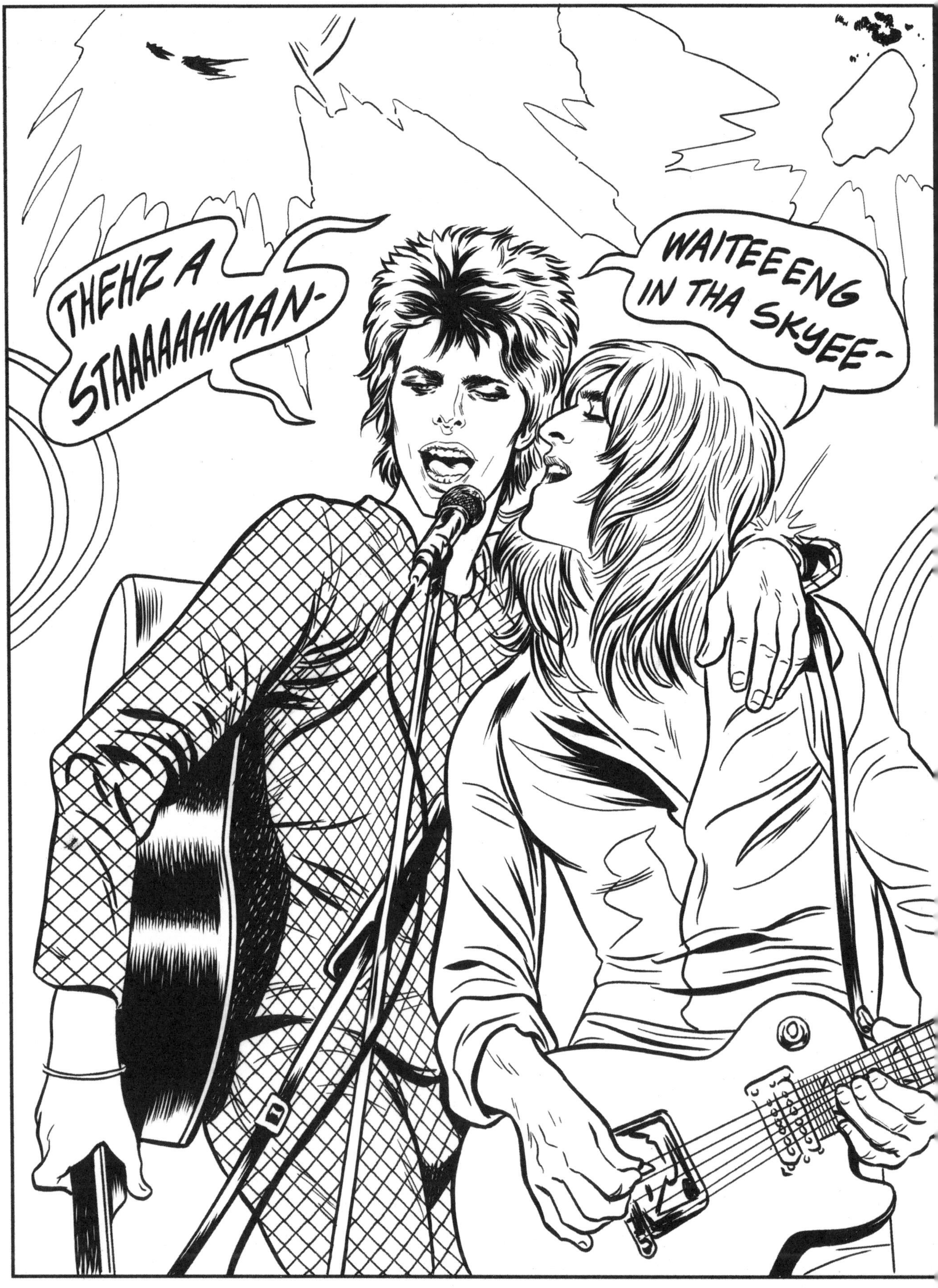
THEHZ A STAAAAAHMAN-
WAITEEENG IN THA SKYEE-

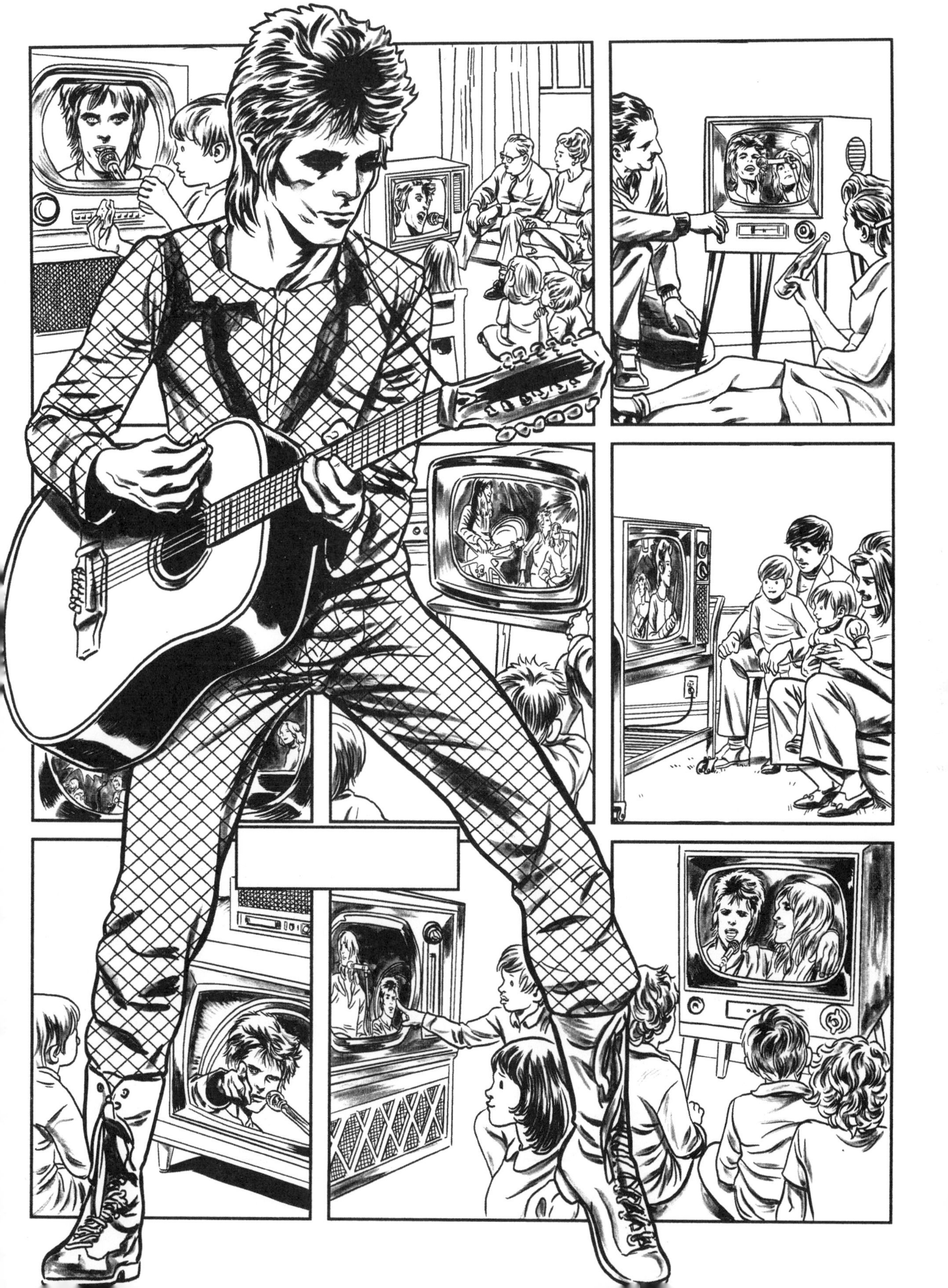

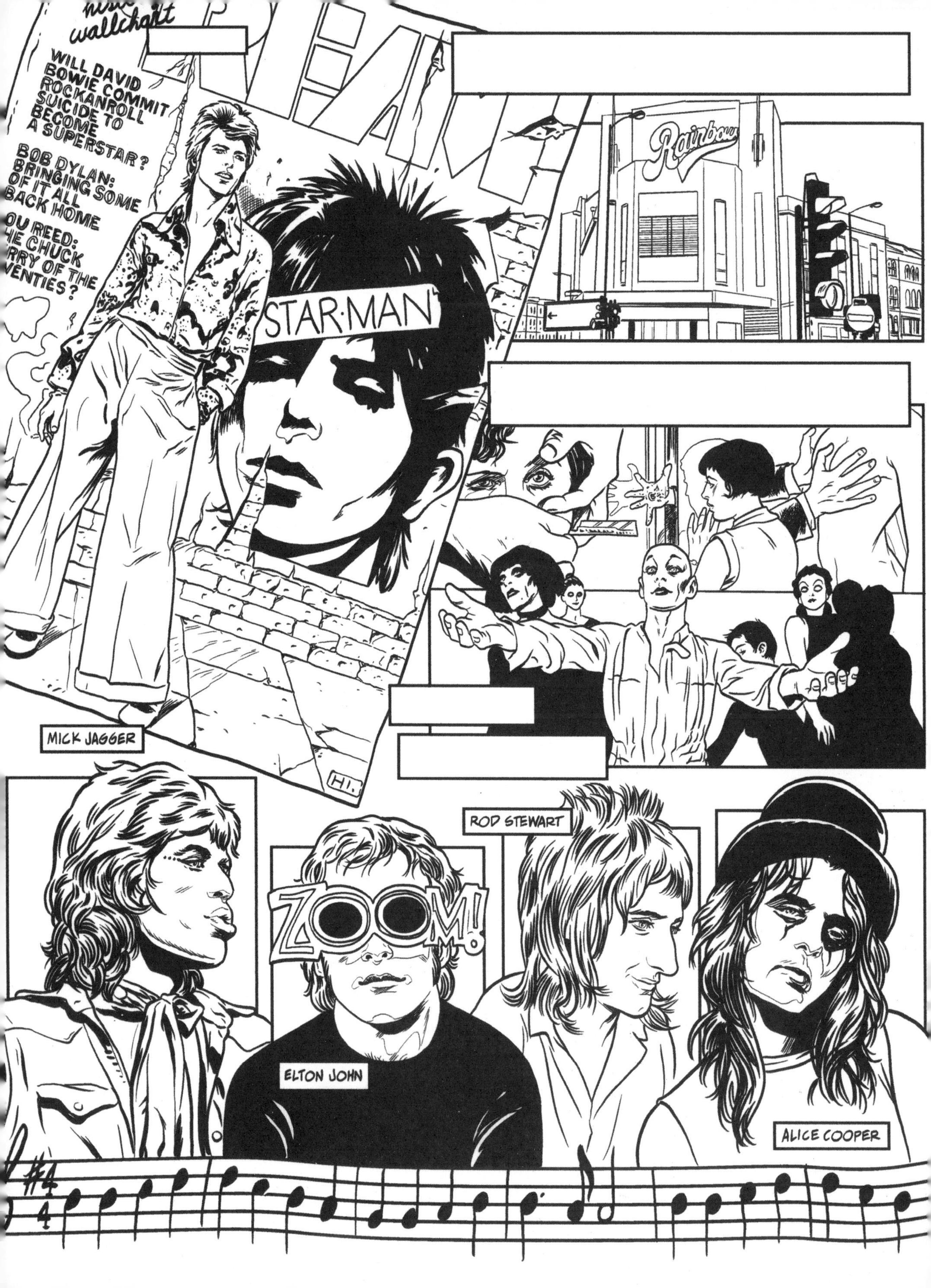
wallchart
WILL DAVID BOWIE COMMIT ROCKANROLL SUICIDE TO BECOME A SUPERSTAR?
BOB DYLAN: BRINGING SOME OF IT ALL BACK HOME
OU REED: HE CHUCK RRY OF THE VENTIES?
STAR·MAN
Rainbow
MICK JAGGER
ZOOM!
ROD STEWART
ELTON JOHN
ALICE COOPER

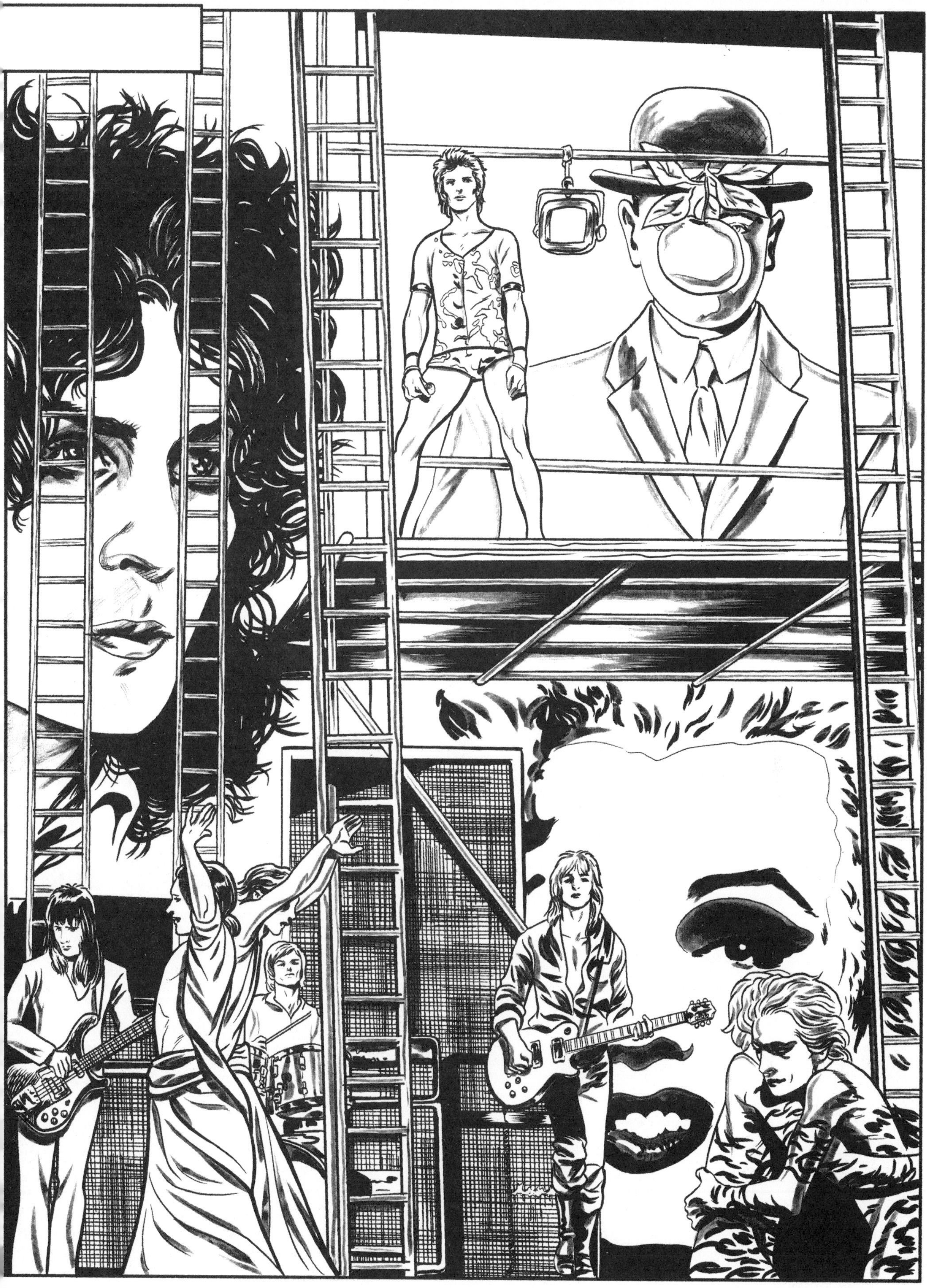

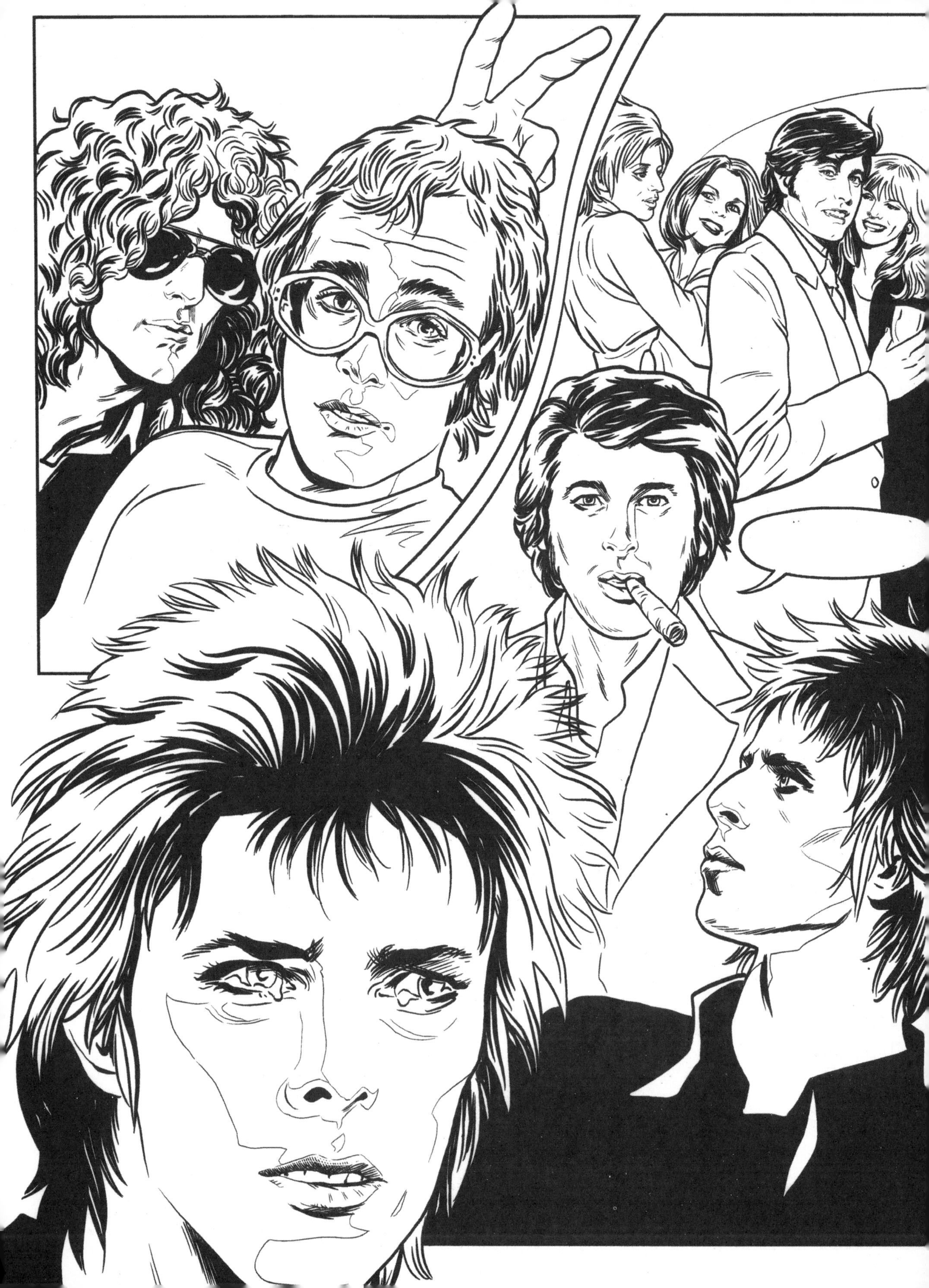

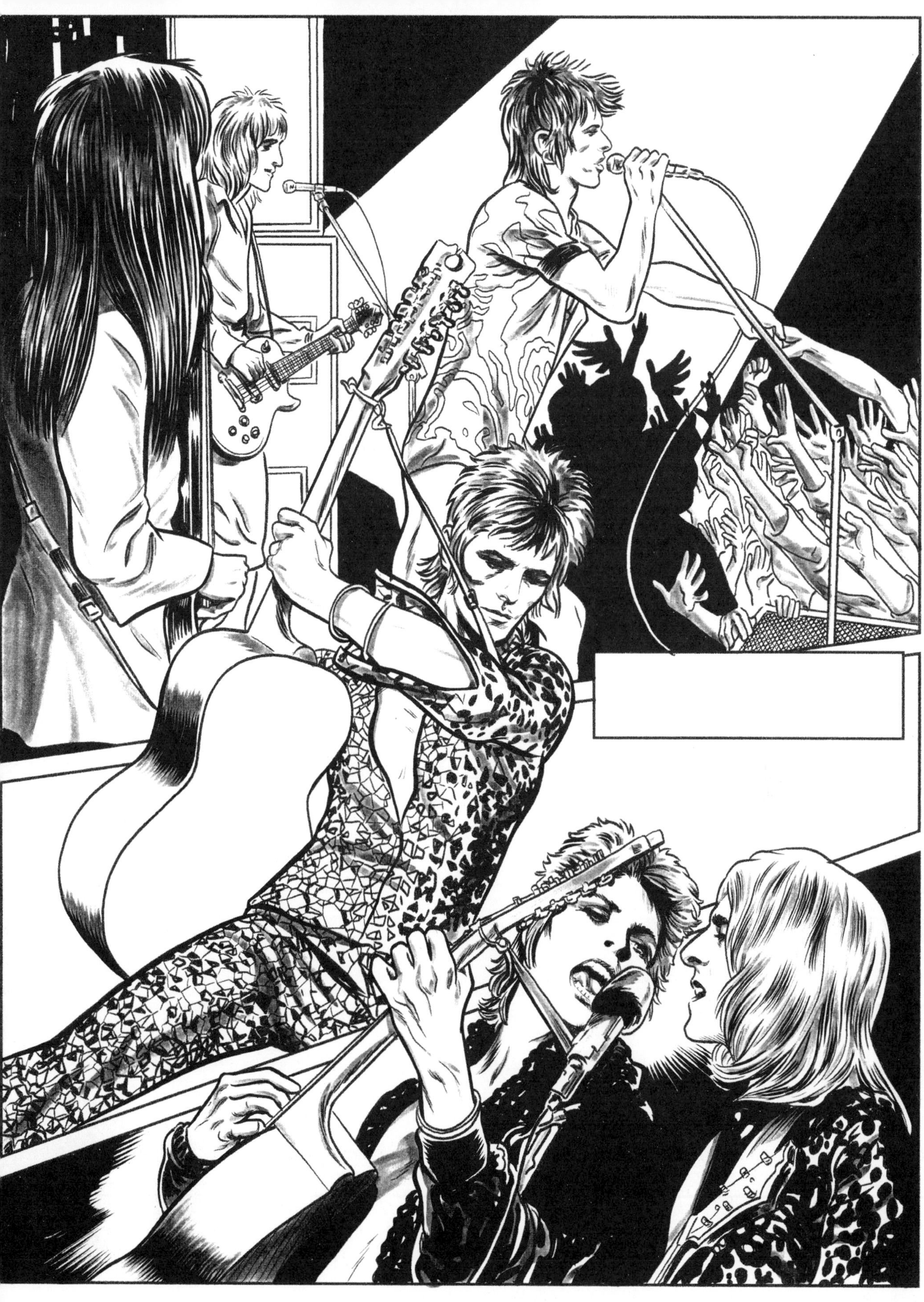

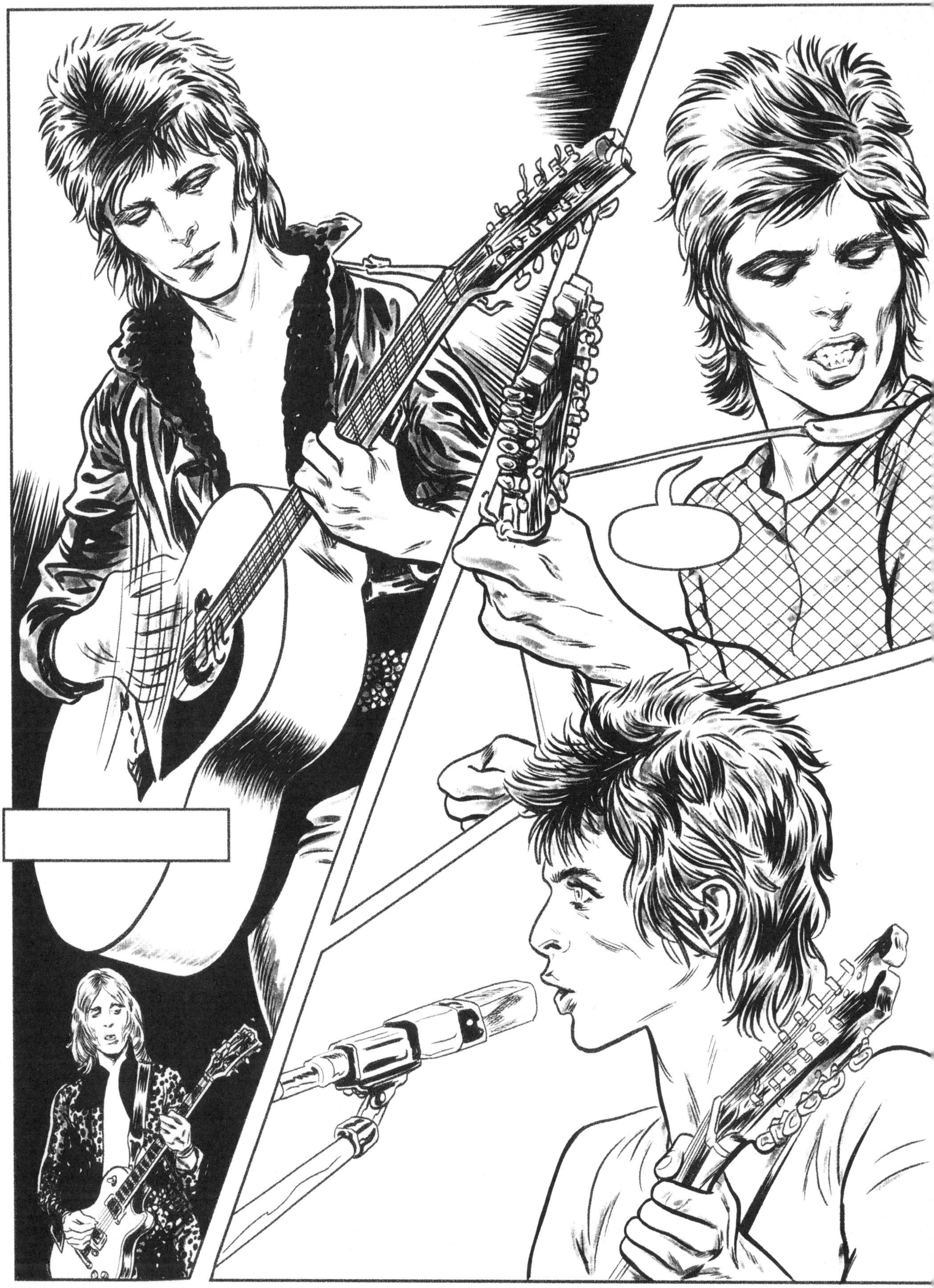

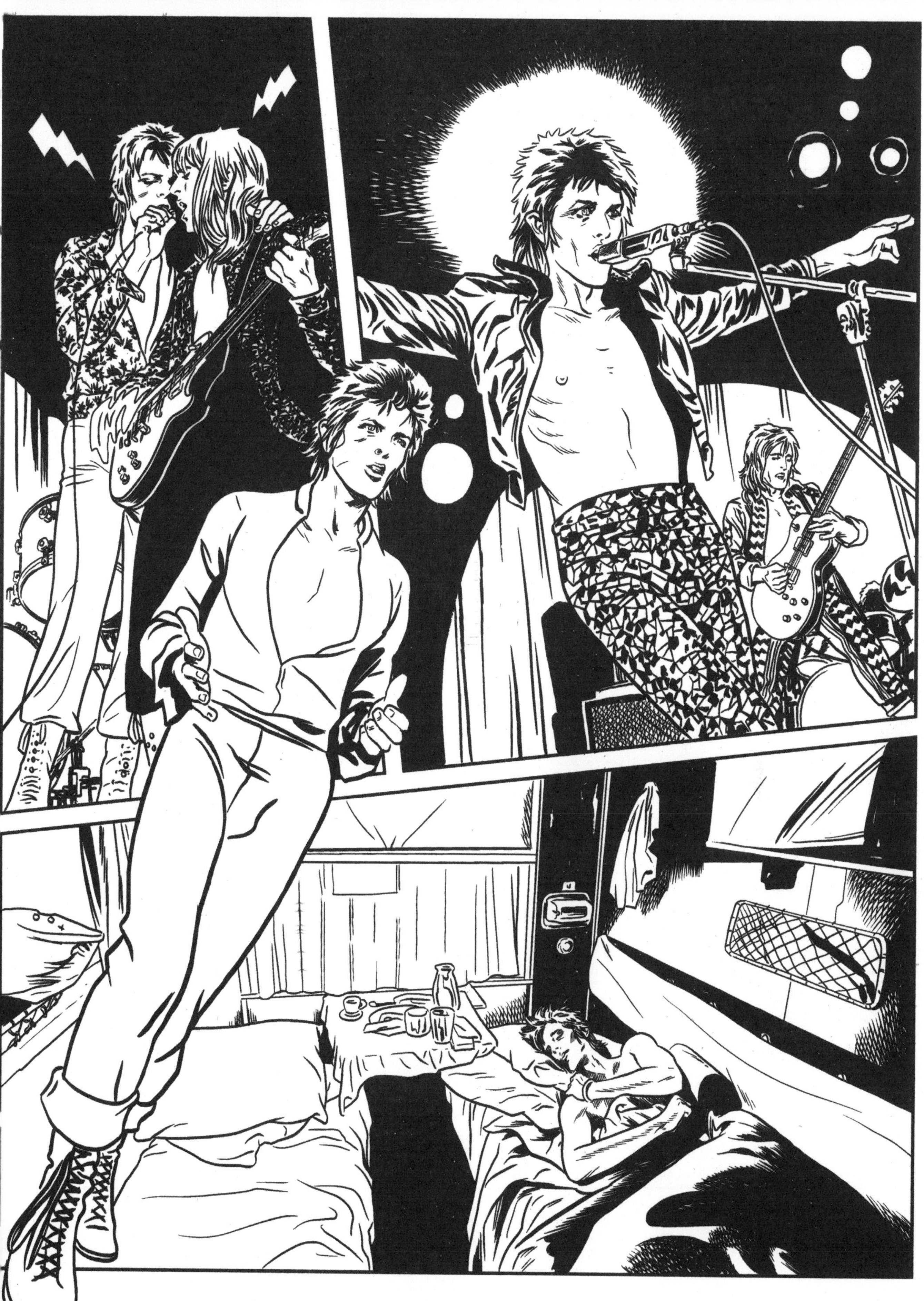

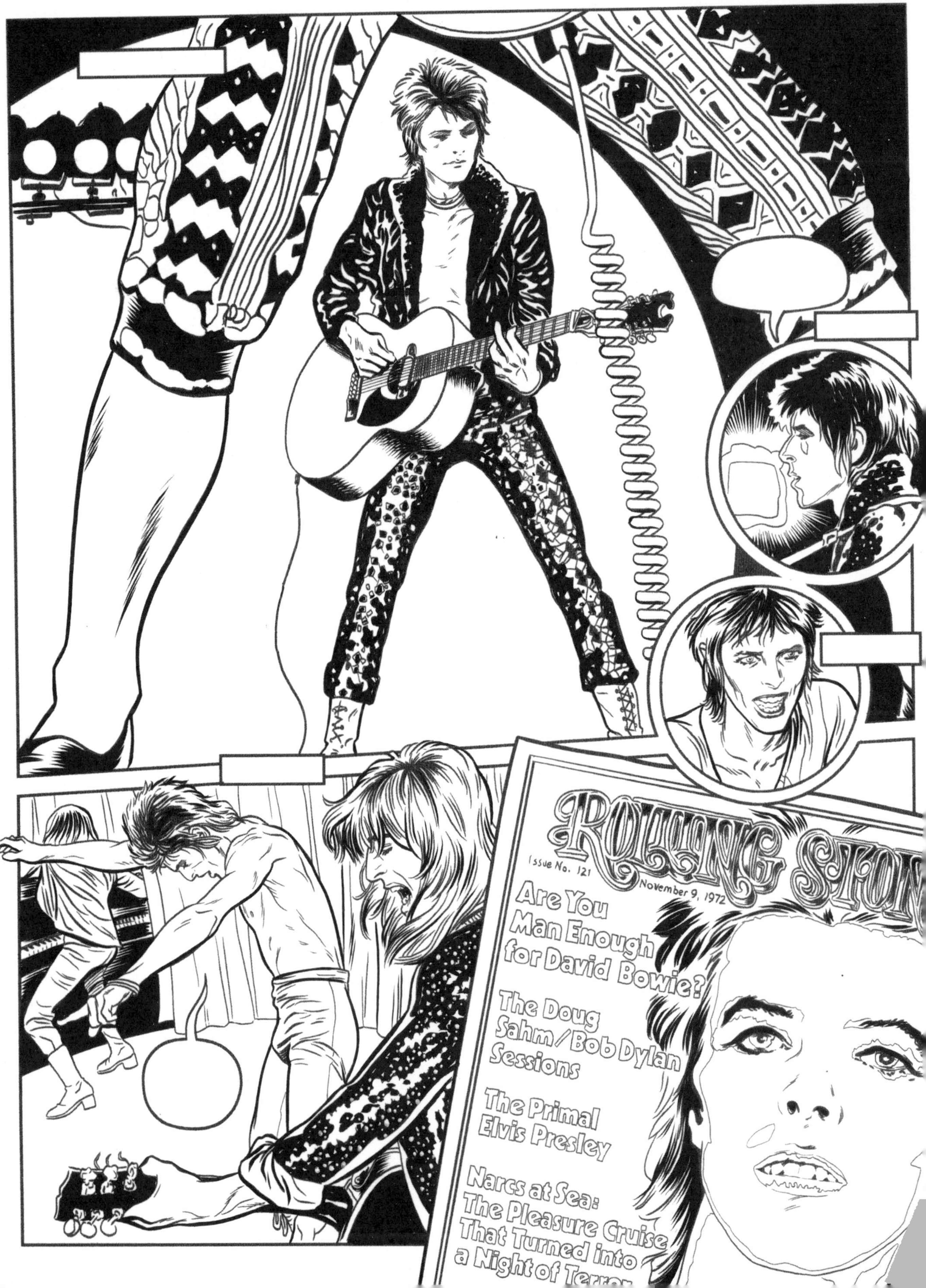
Issue No. 121
November 9, 1972
Are You Man Enough for David Bowie?
The Doug Sahm/Bob Dylan Sessions
The Primal Elvis Presley
Narcs at Sea: The Pleasure Cruise That Turned into a Night of

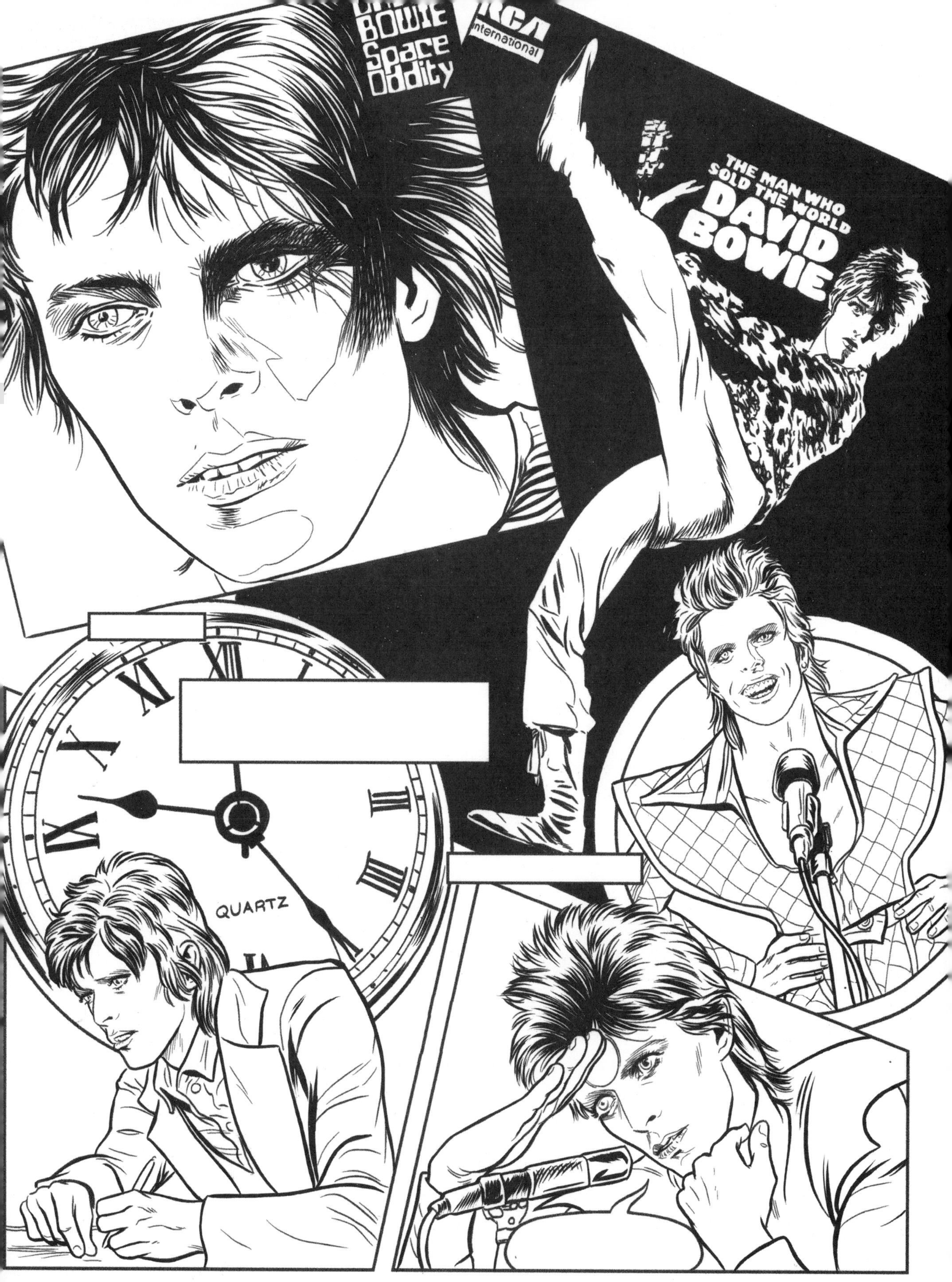
BOWIE
Space Oddity
RCA International
THE MAN WHO SOLD THE WORLD
DAVID BOWIE
QUARTZ

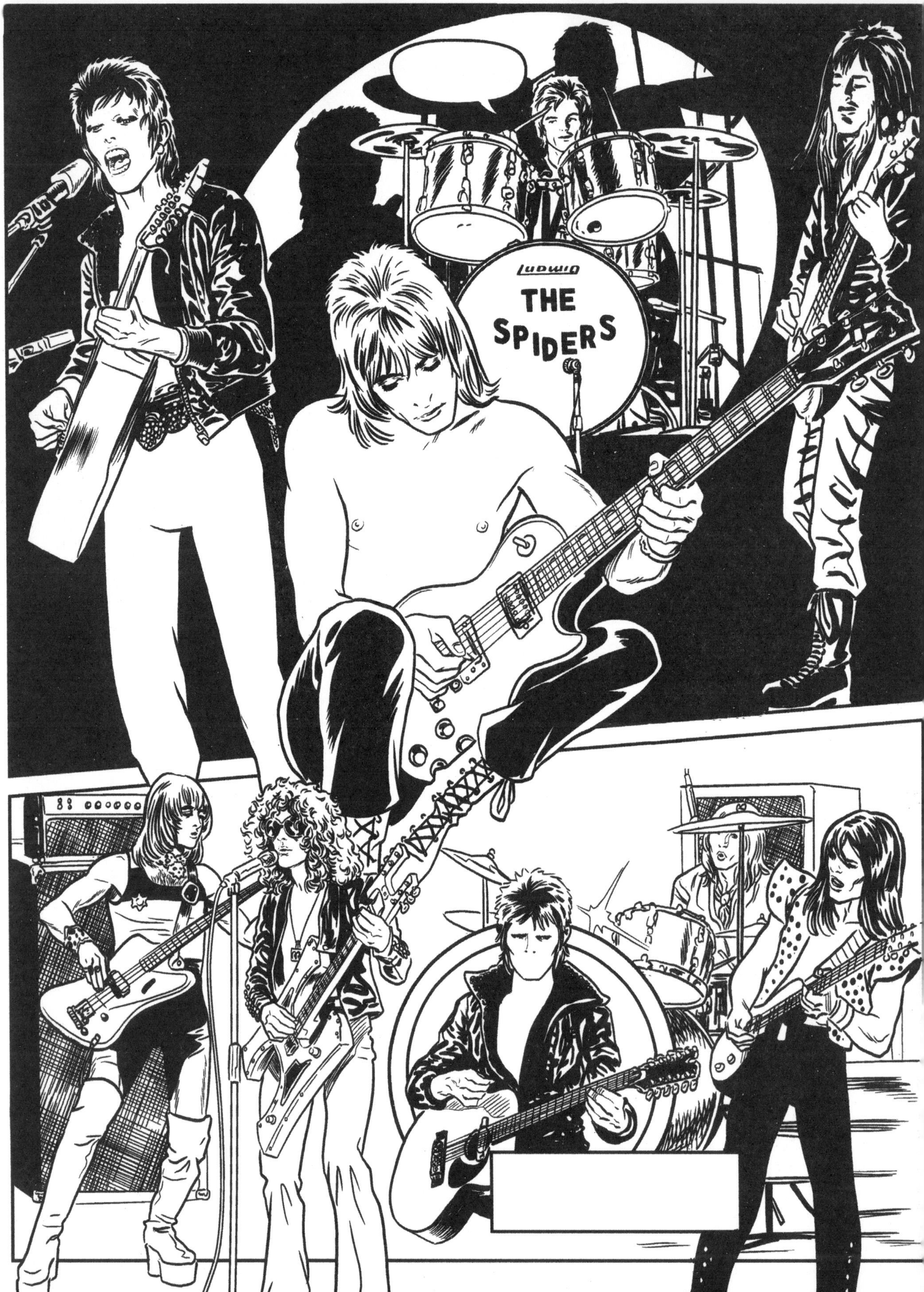
LUDWIG
THE SPIDERS

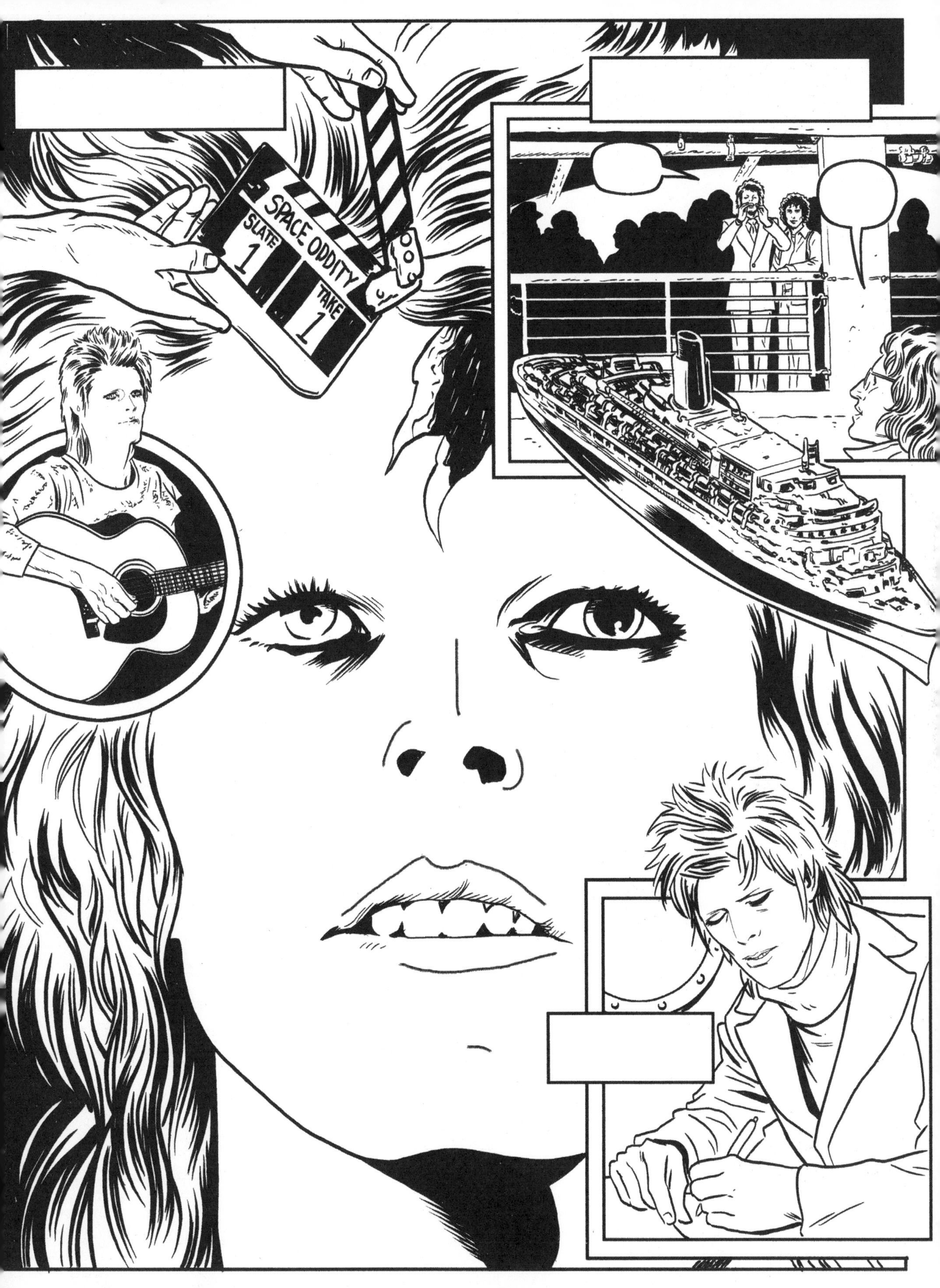
SPACE ODDITY
SLATE 1
TAKE 1

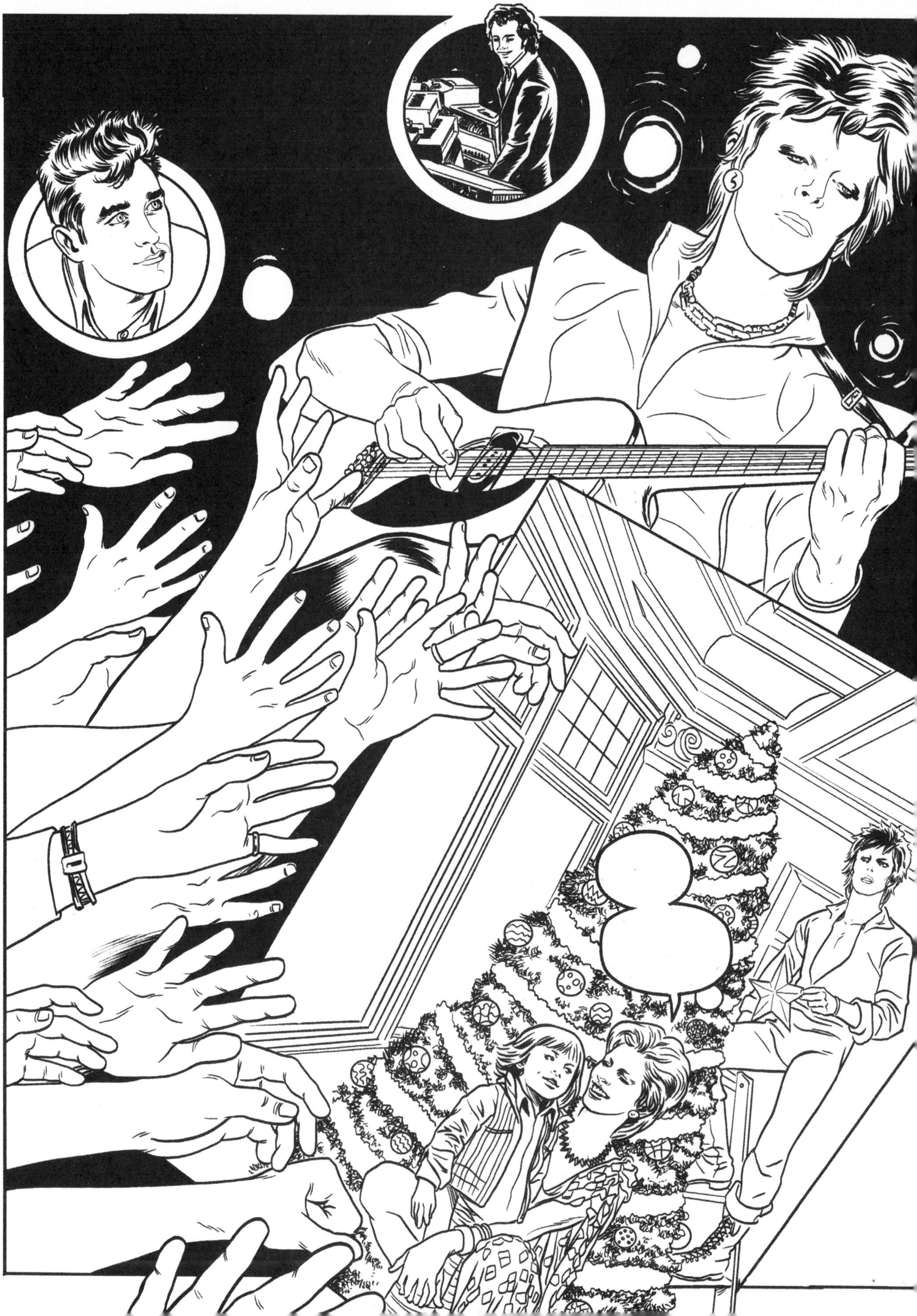

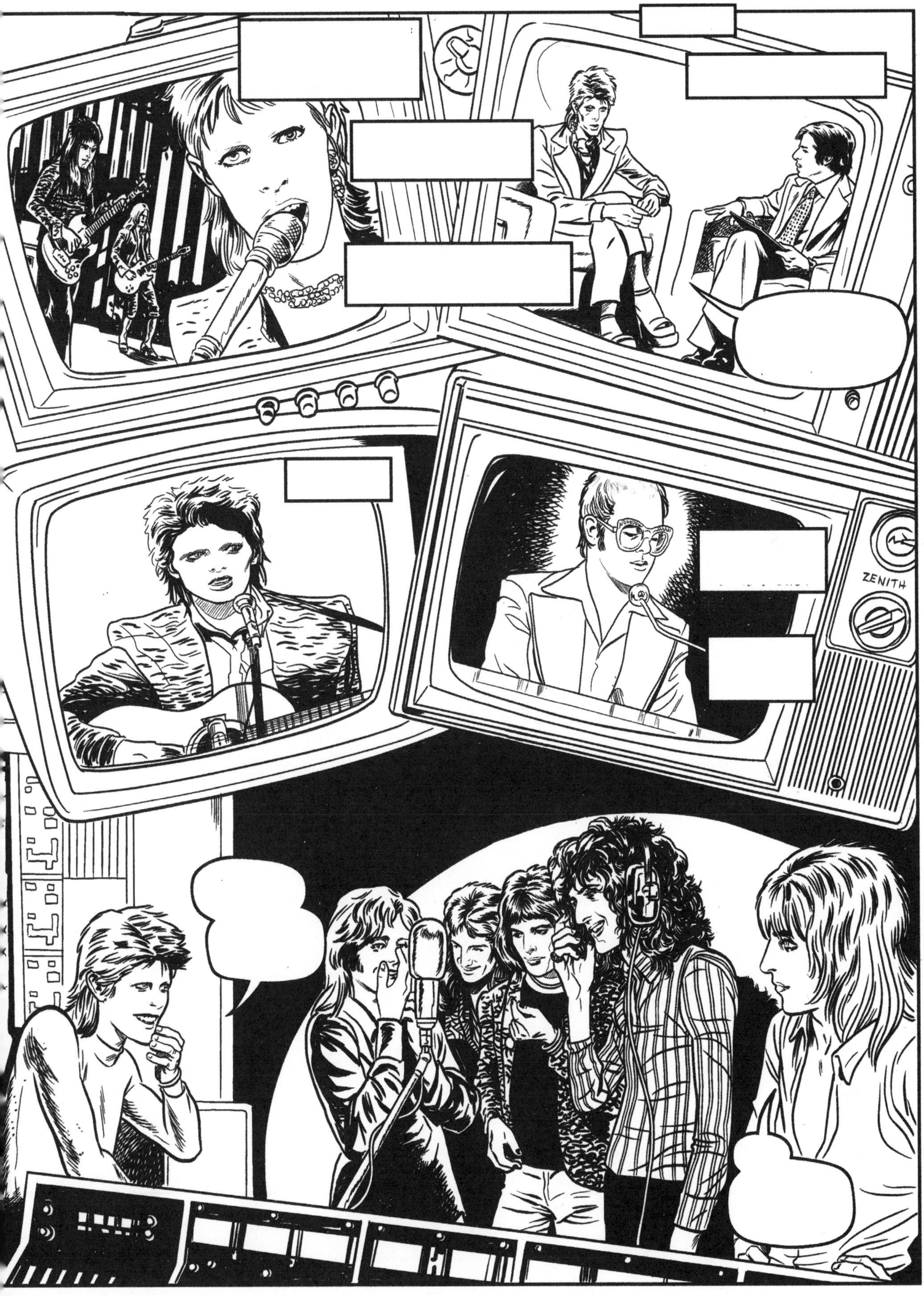
ZENITH

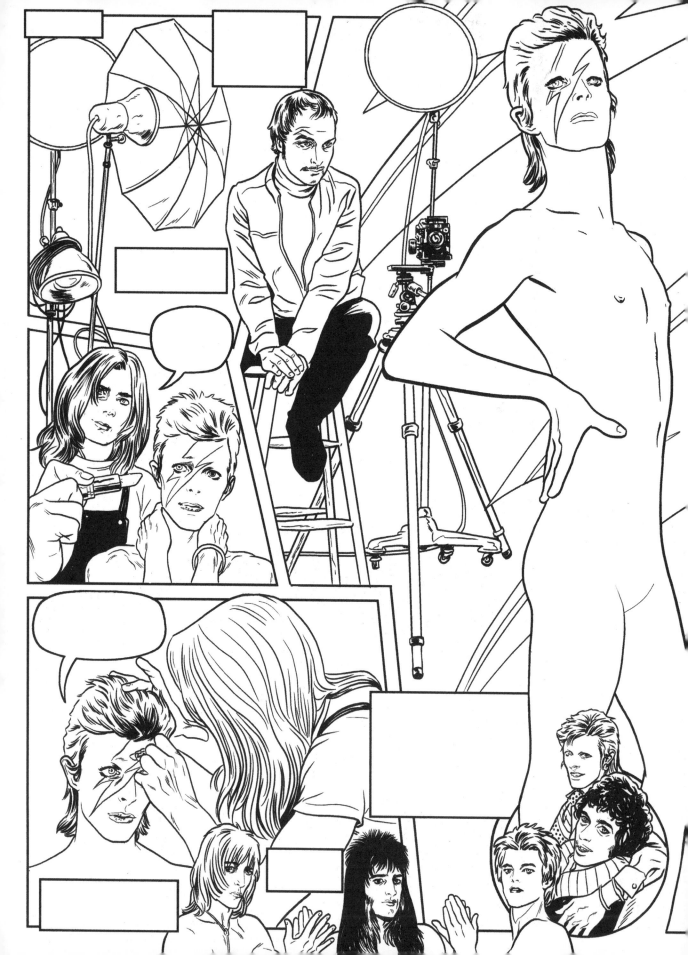

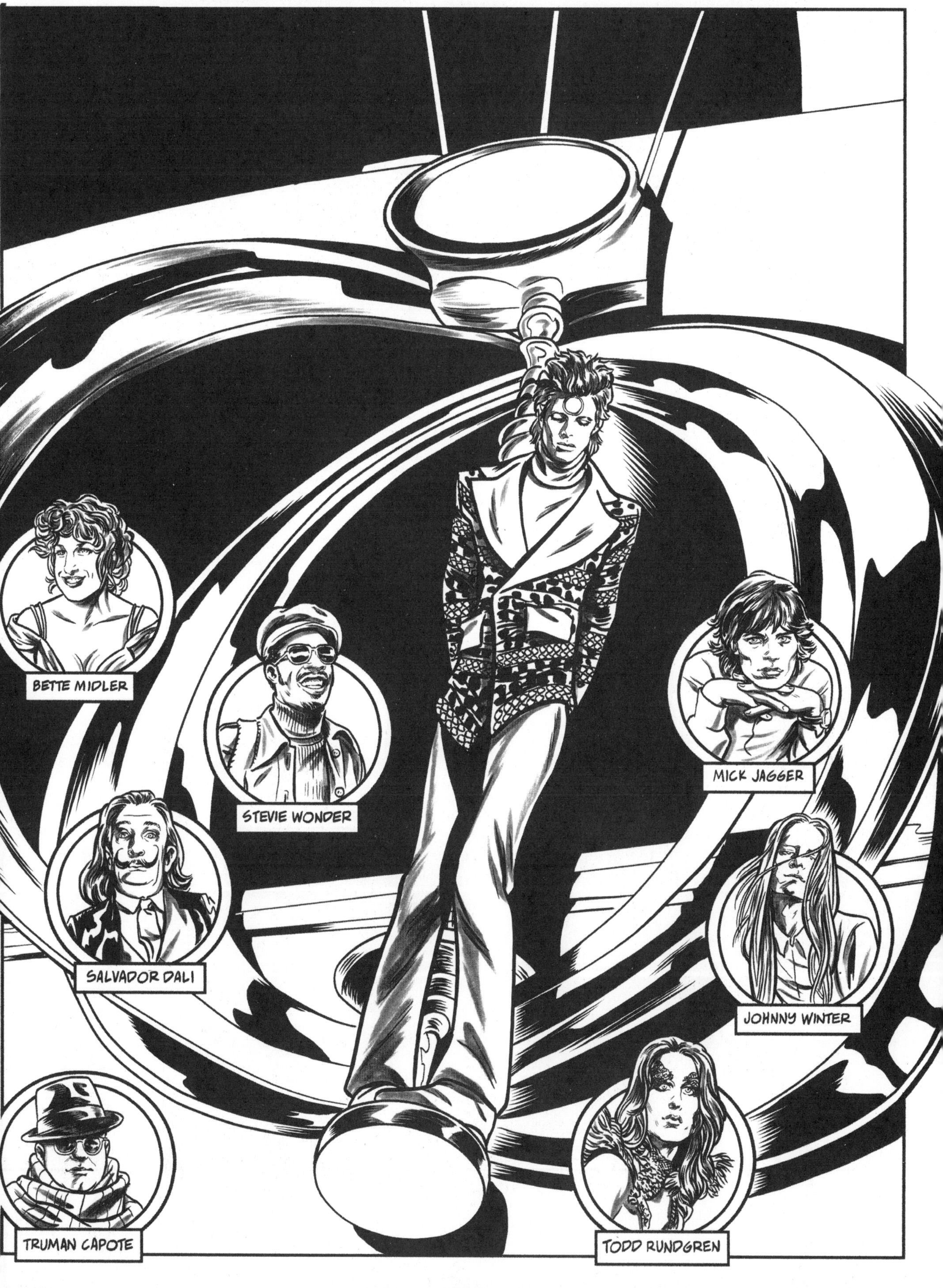
BETTE MIDLER
STEVIE WONDER
MICK JAGGER
SALVADOR DALI
JOHNNY WINTER
TRUMAN CAPOTE
TODD RUNDGREN

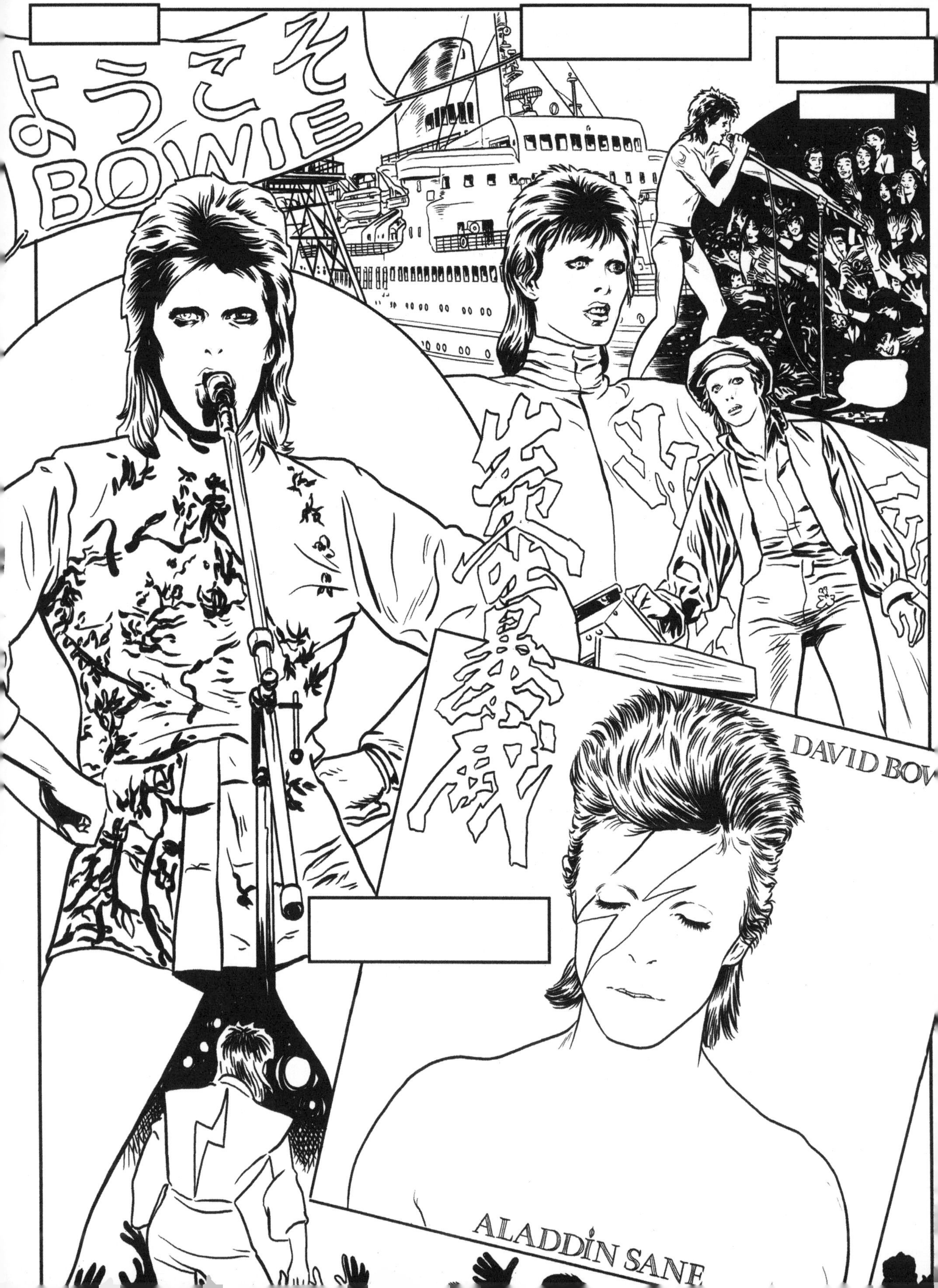
ようこそ
BOWIE
DAVID BOW
ALADDIN SANE

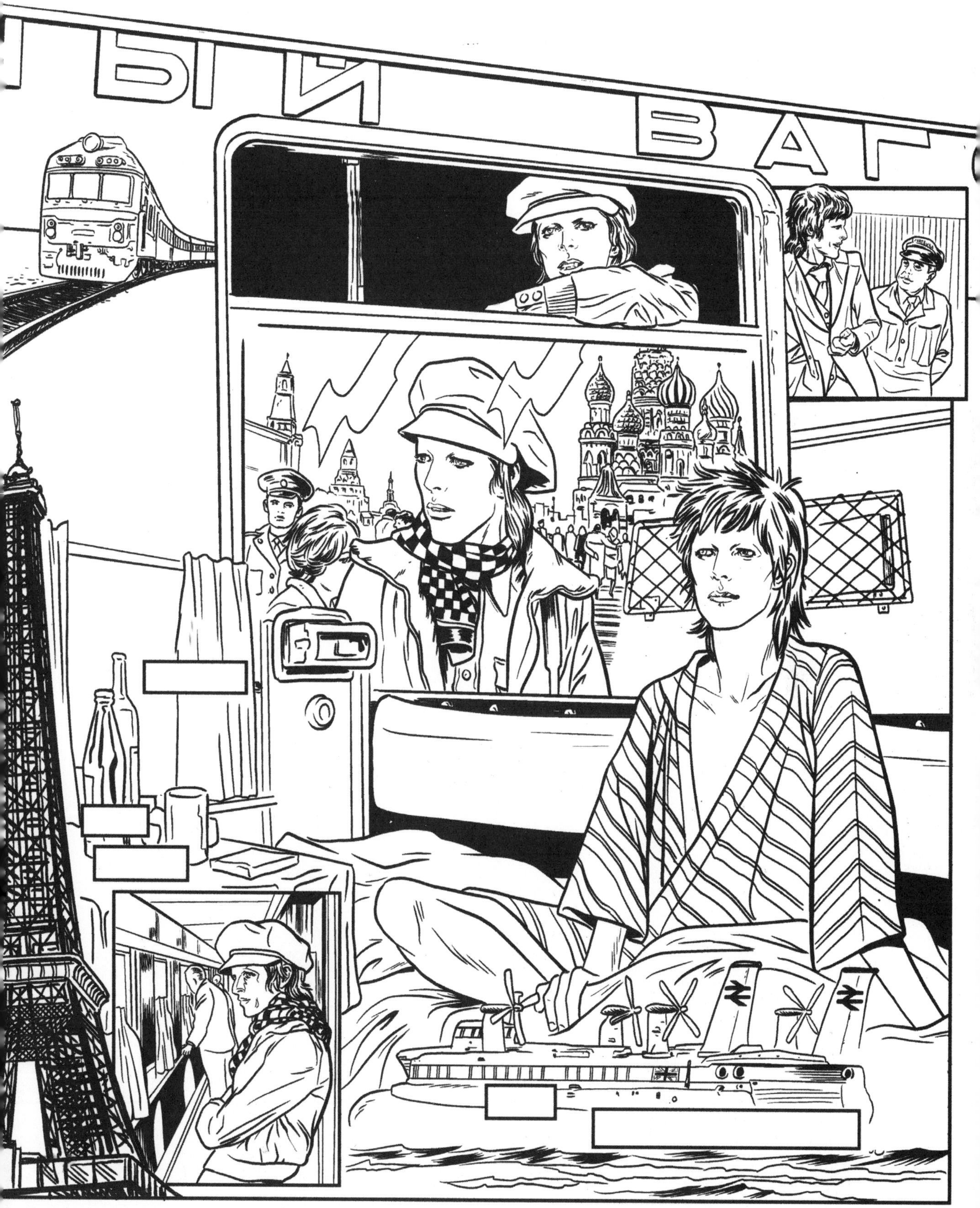
ЫЙ ВАГ

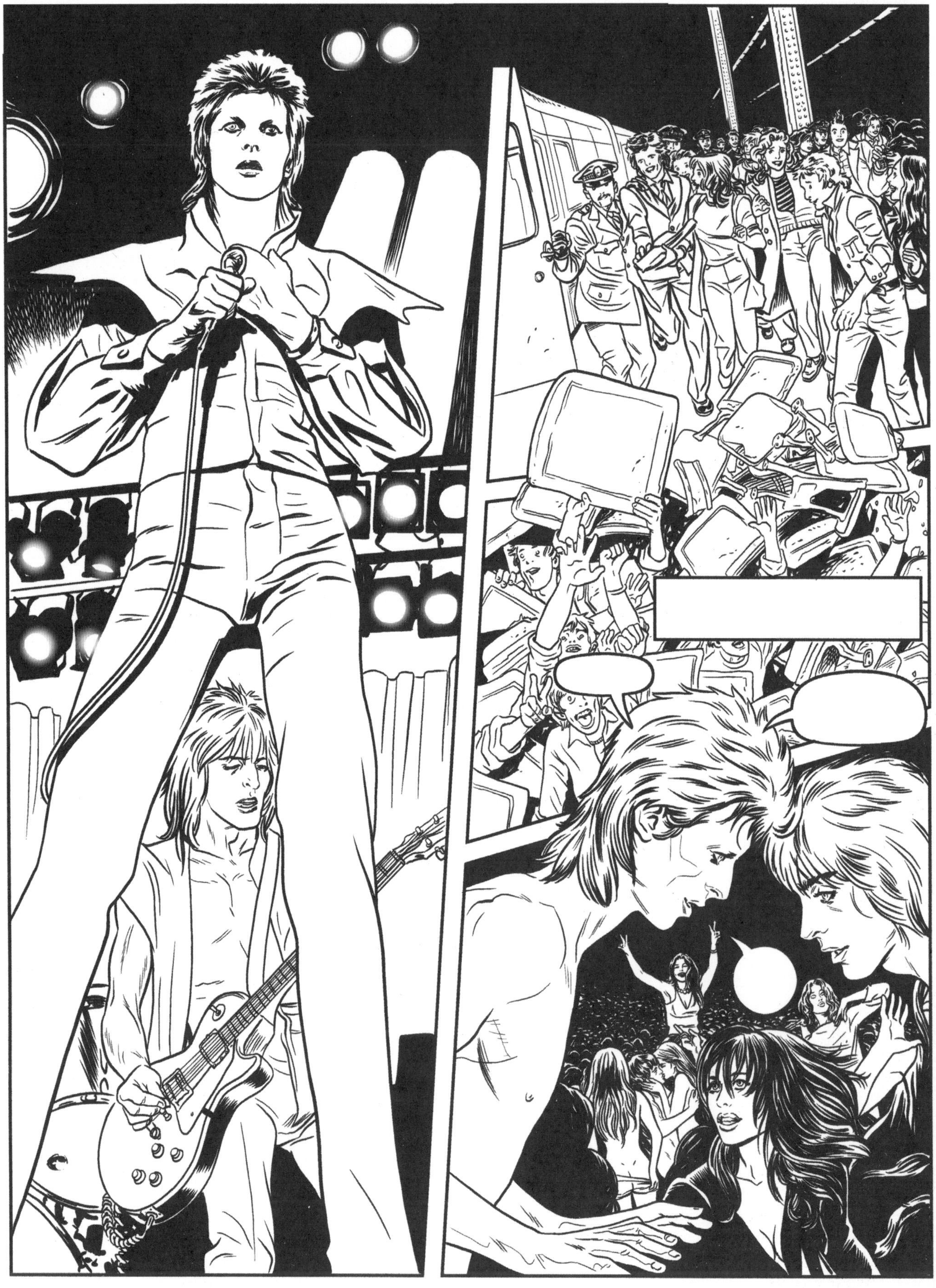

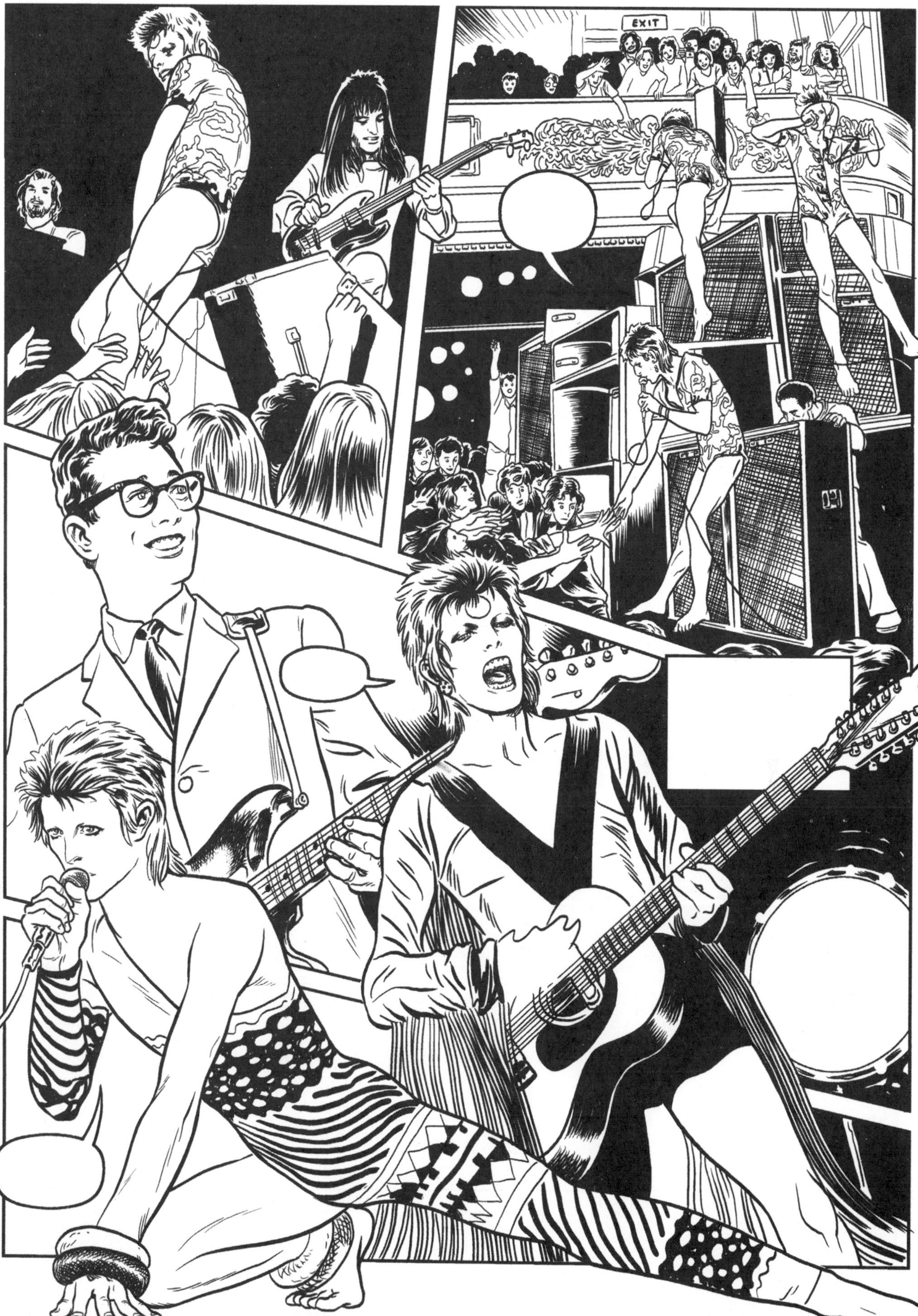
EXIT

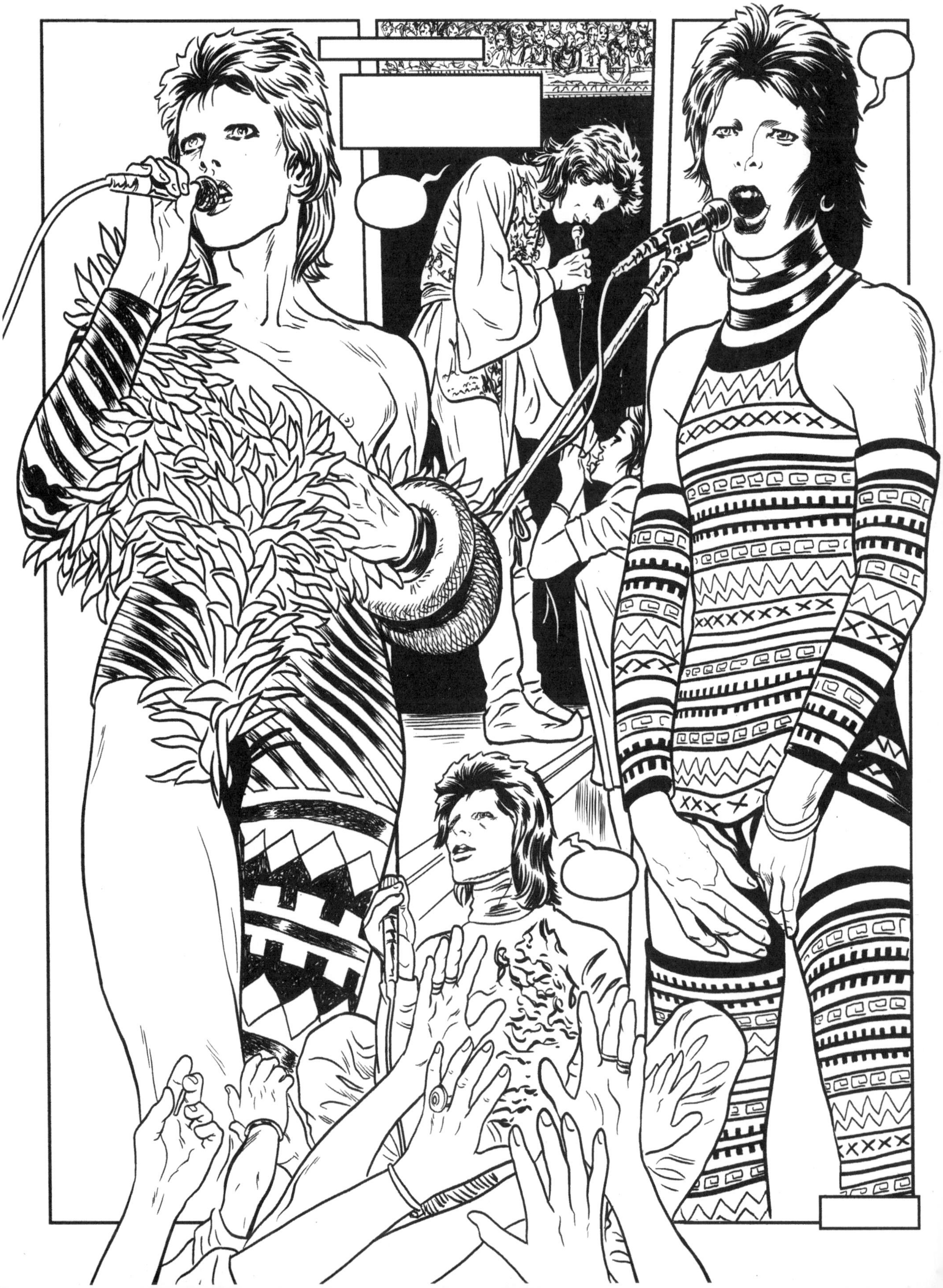

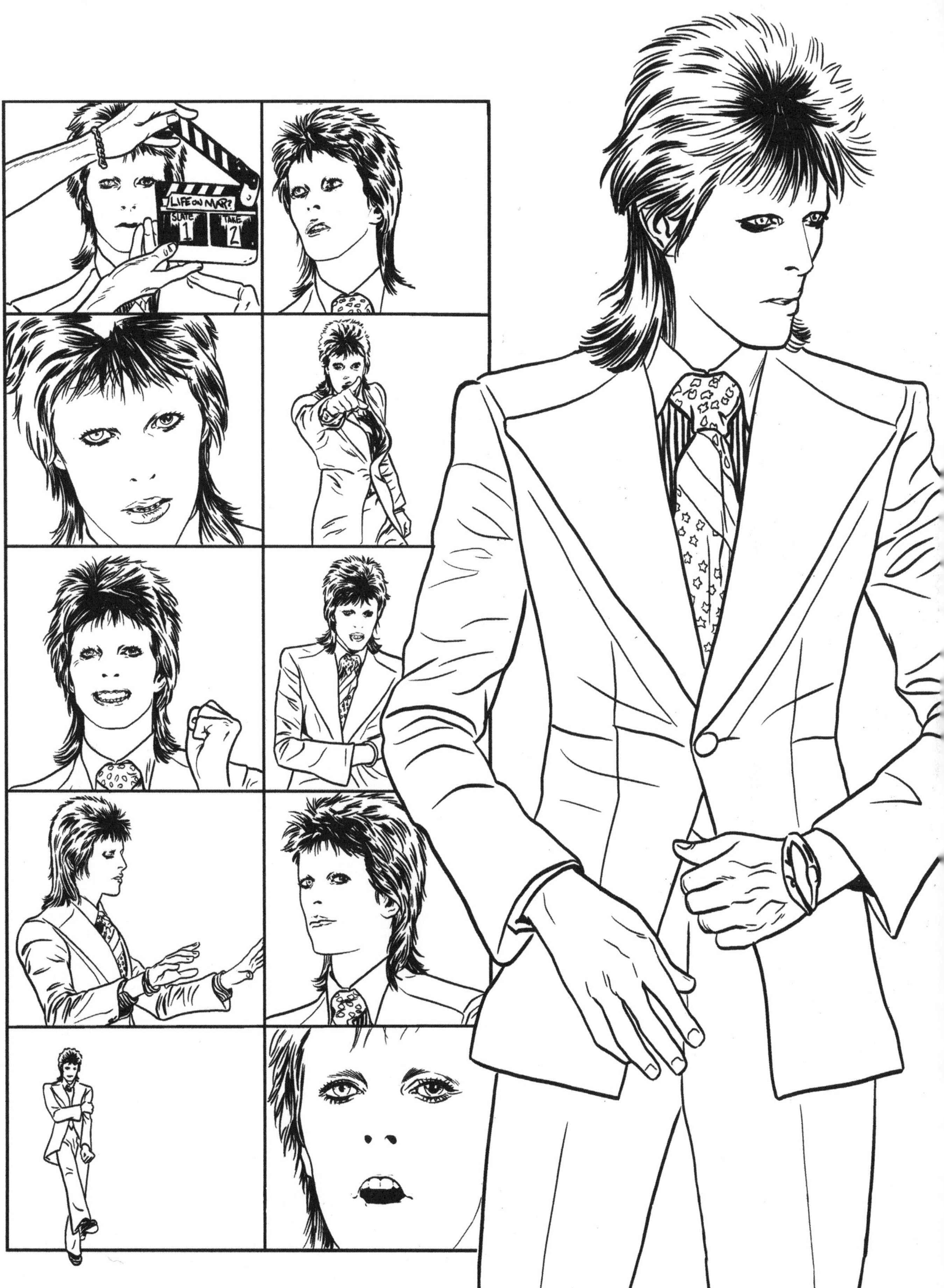
LIFE ON MARS?
SLATE 1
TAKE 2

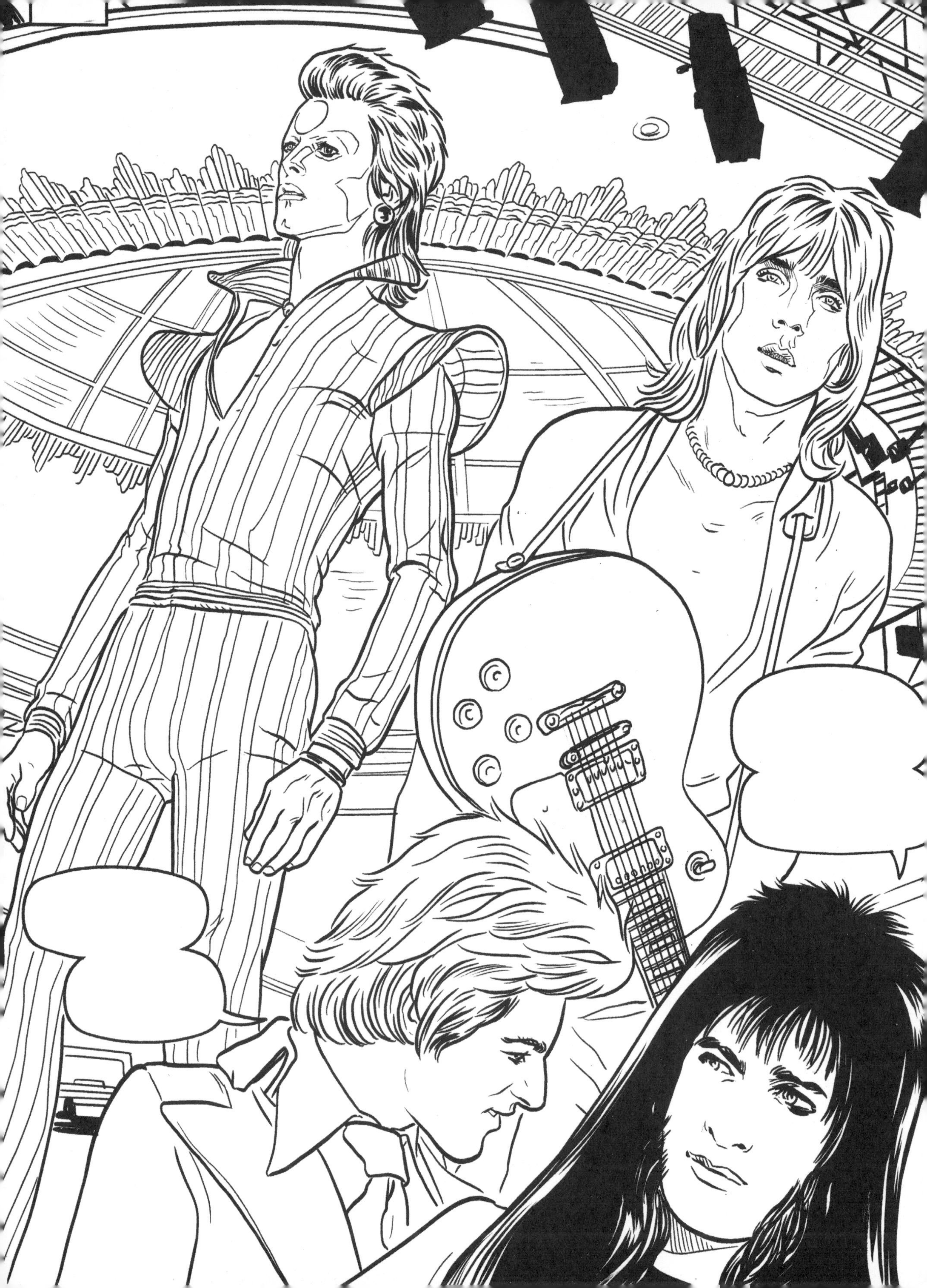

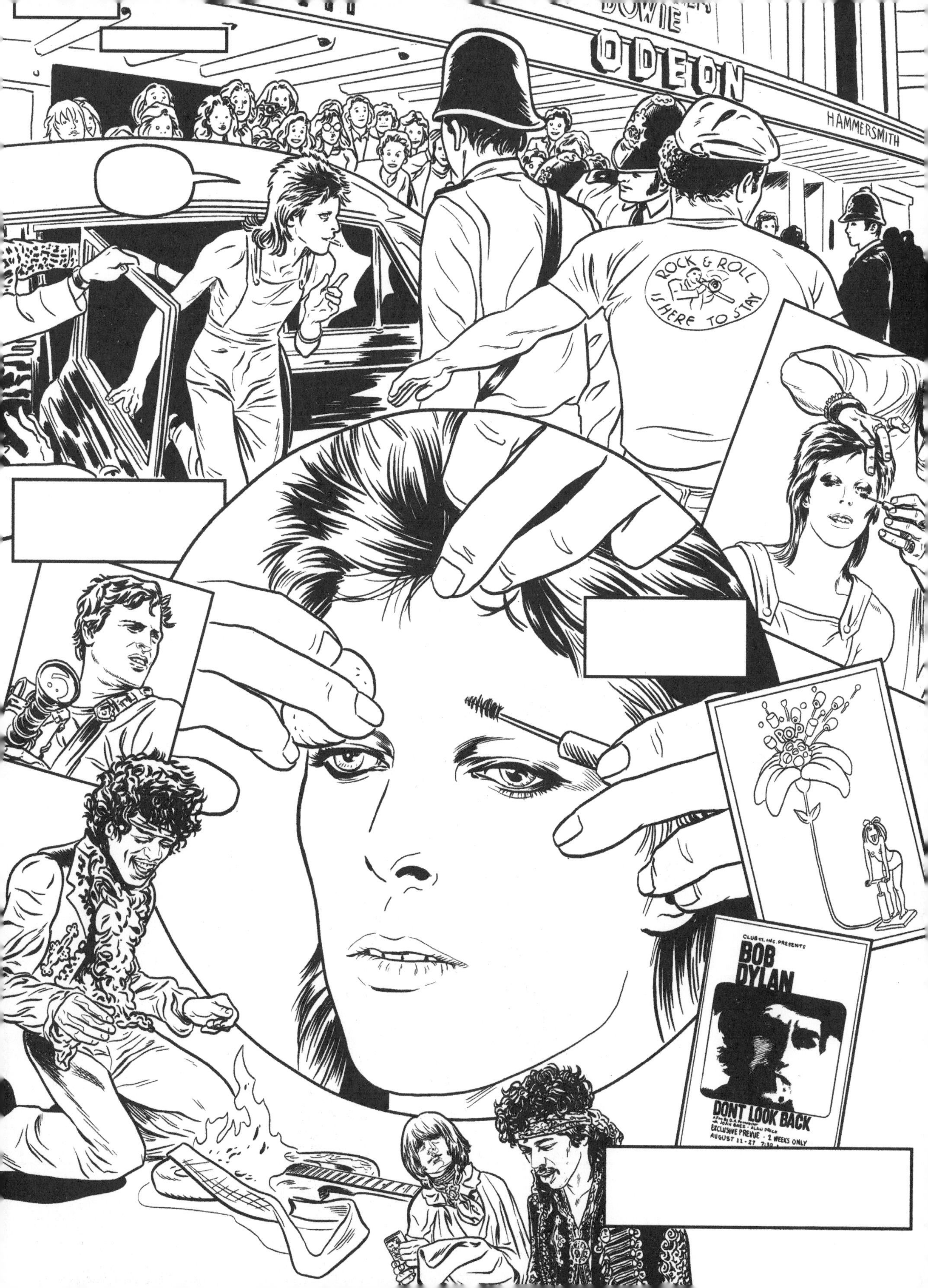
BOWIE
ODEON
HAMMERSMITH
ROCK & ROLL IS HERE TO STAY
POP
CLUB 47, INC. PRESENTS
BOB DYLAN
DONT LOOK BACK
WITH JOAN BAEZ · ALAN PRICE
EXCLUSIVE PREVUE · 2 WEEKS ONLY
AUGUST 11 - 27

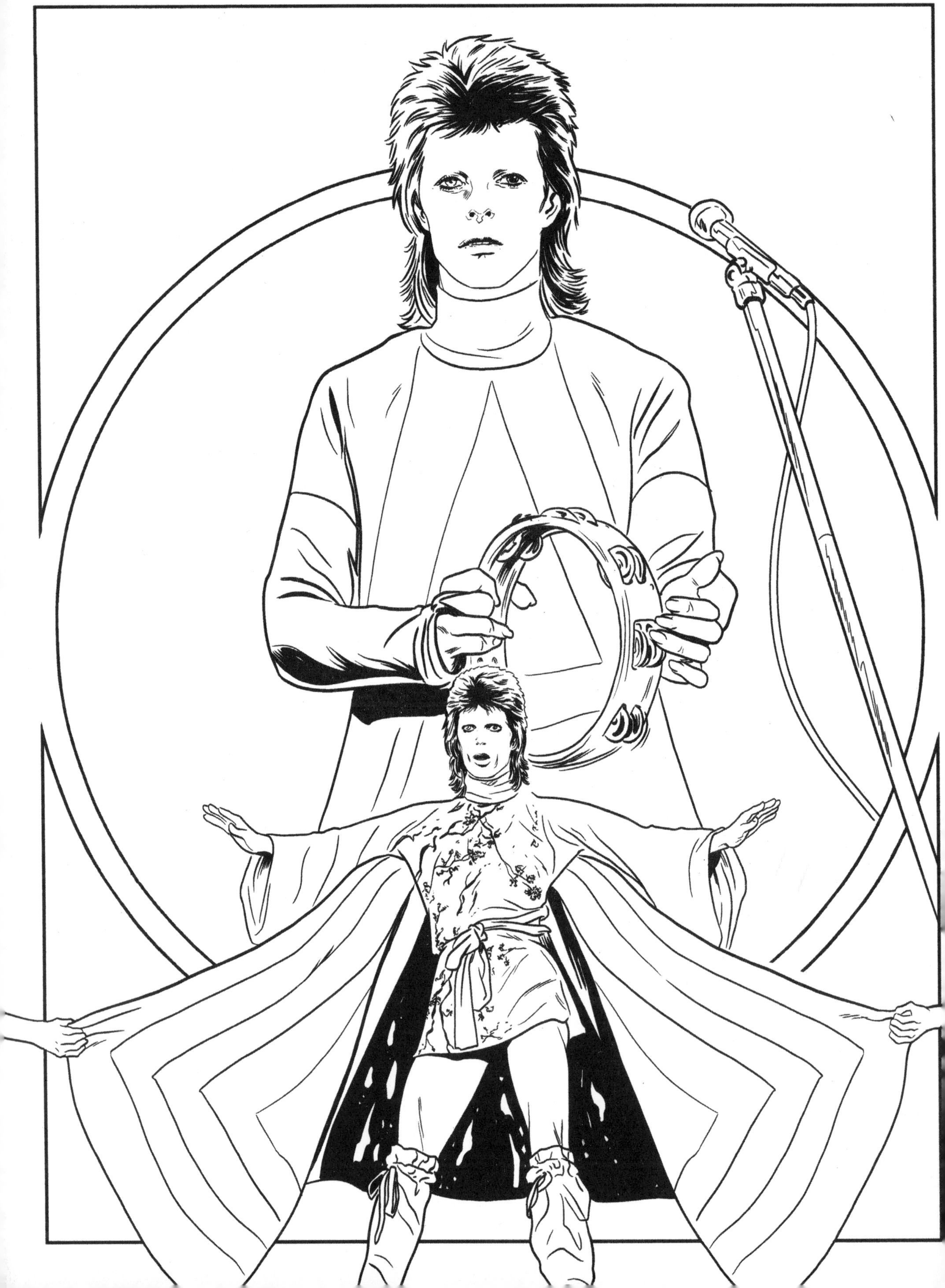

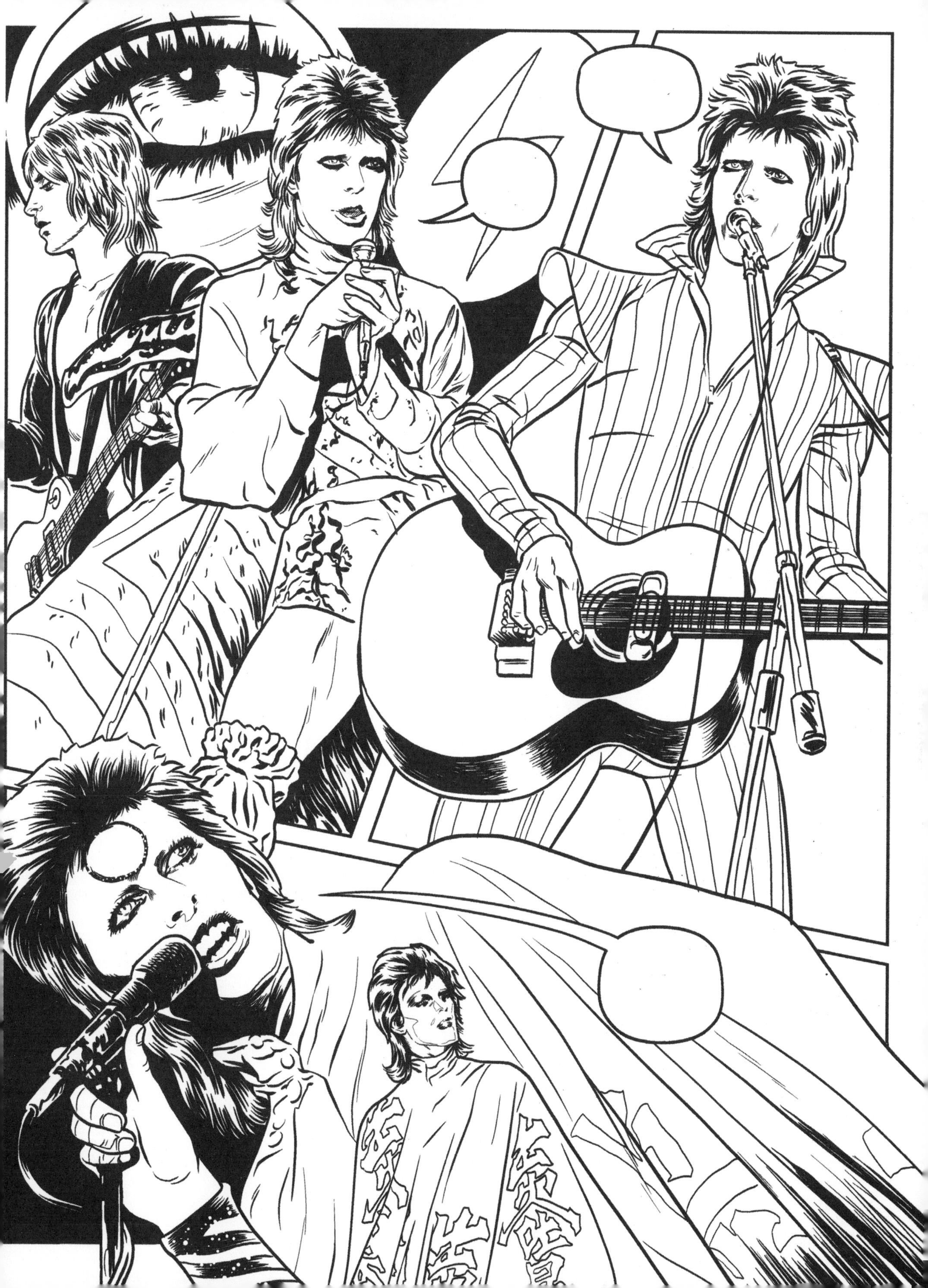

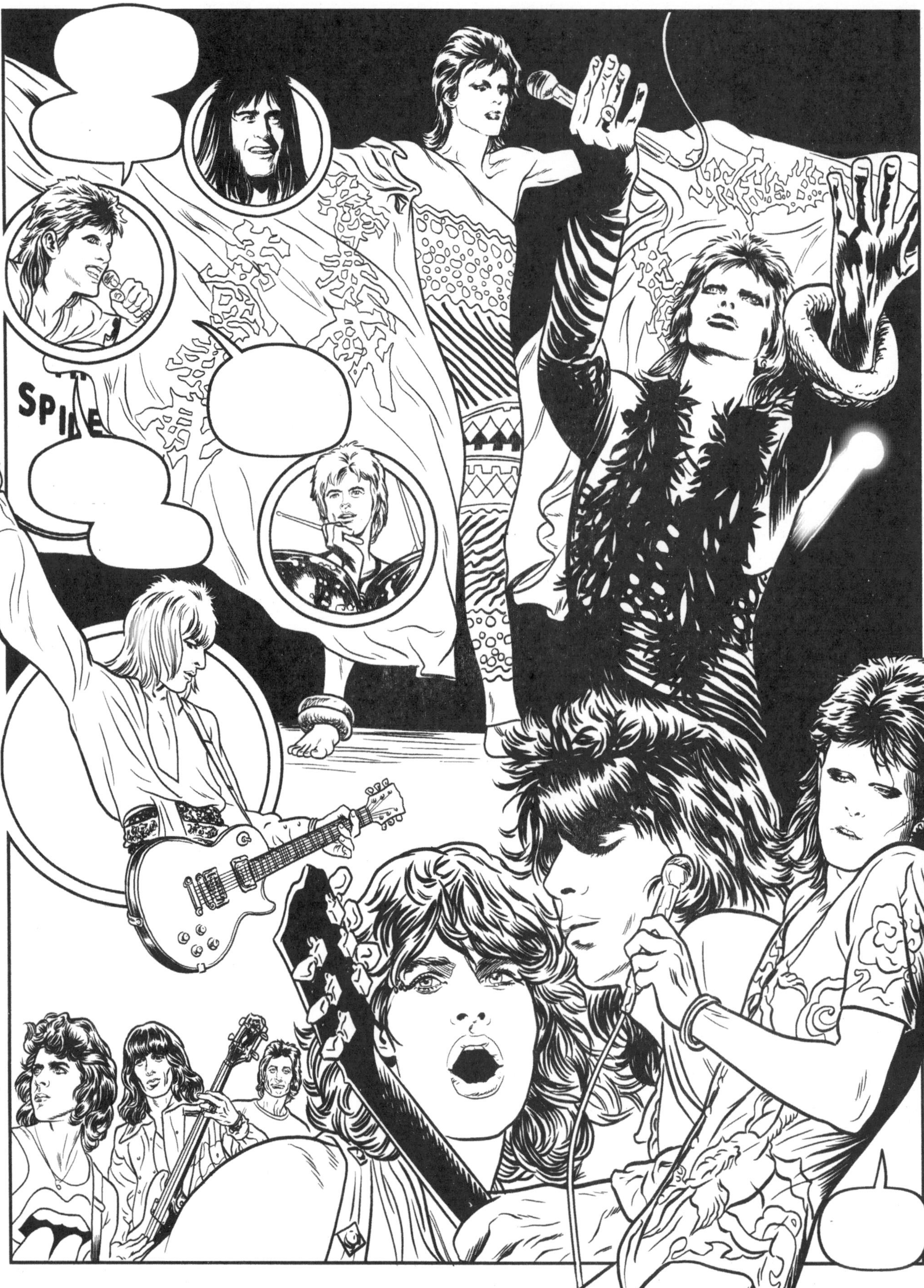
SPIDE

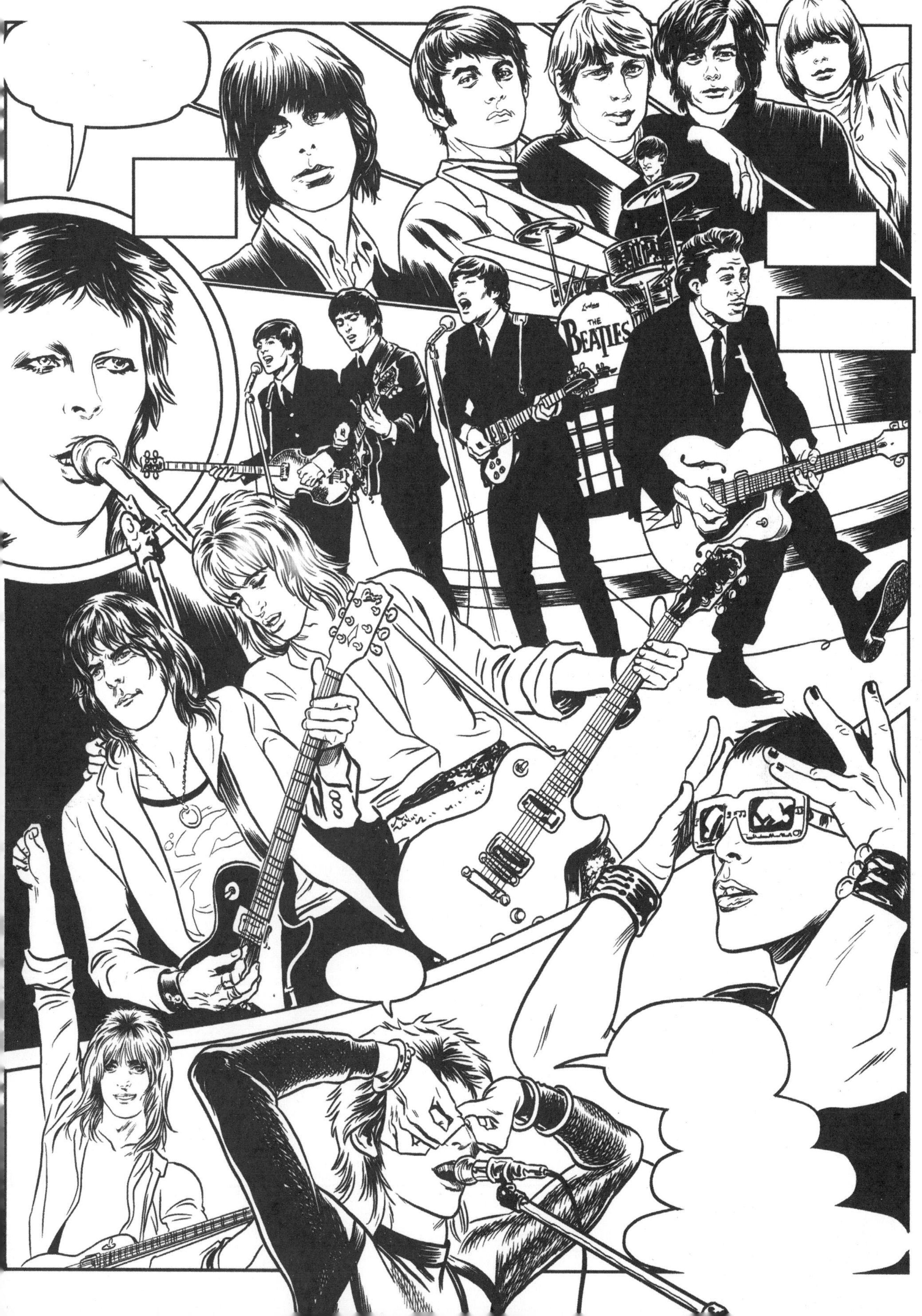
THE BEATLES

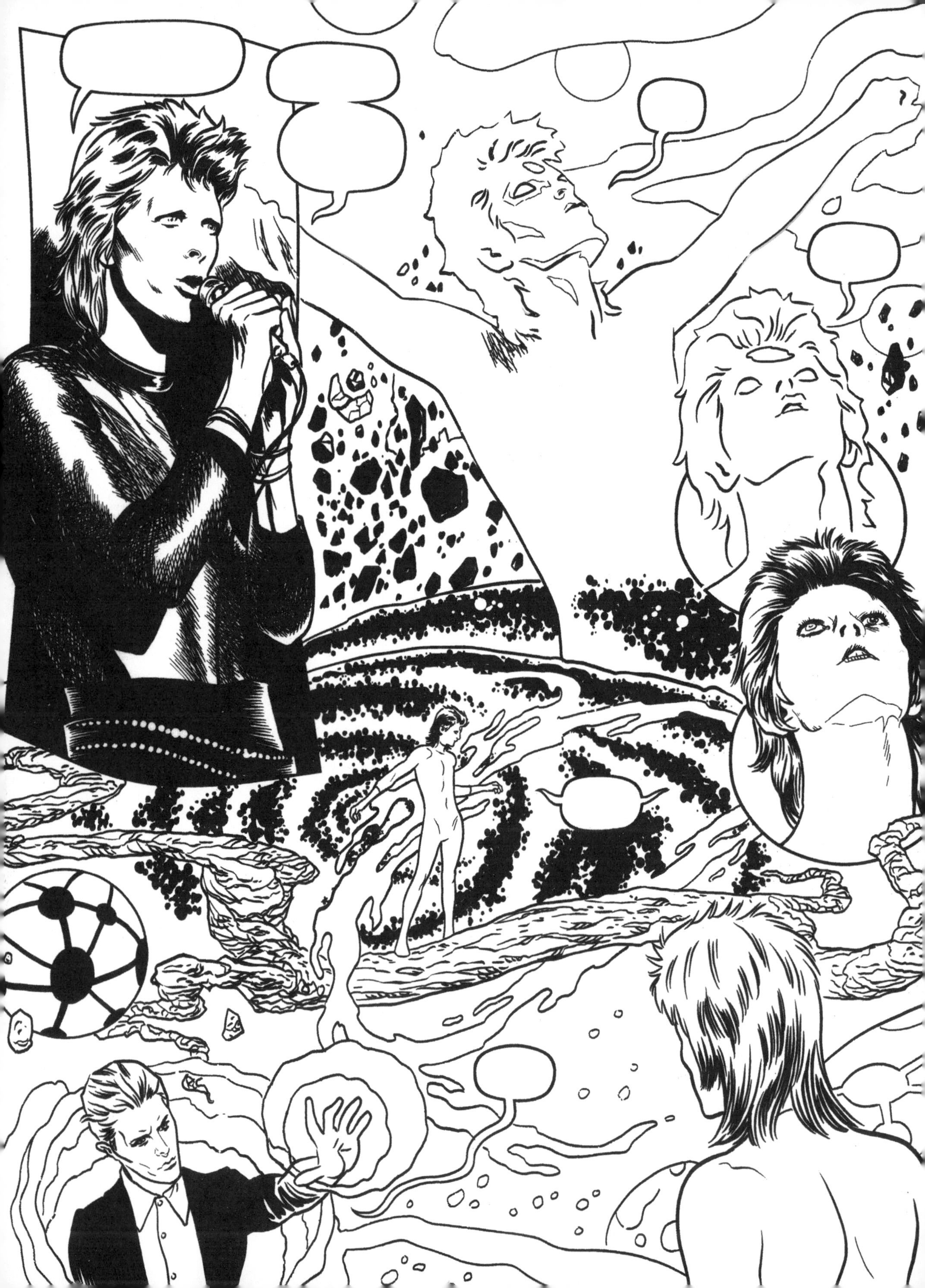

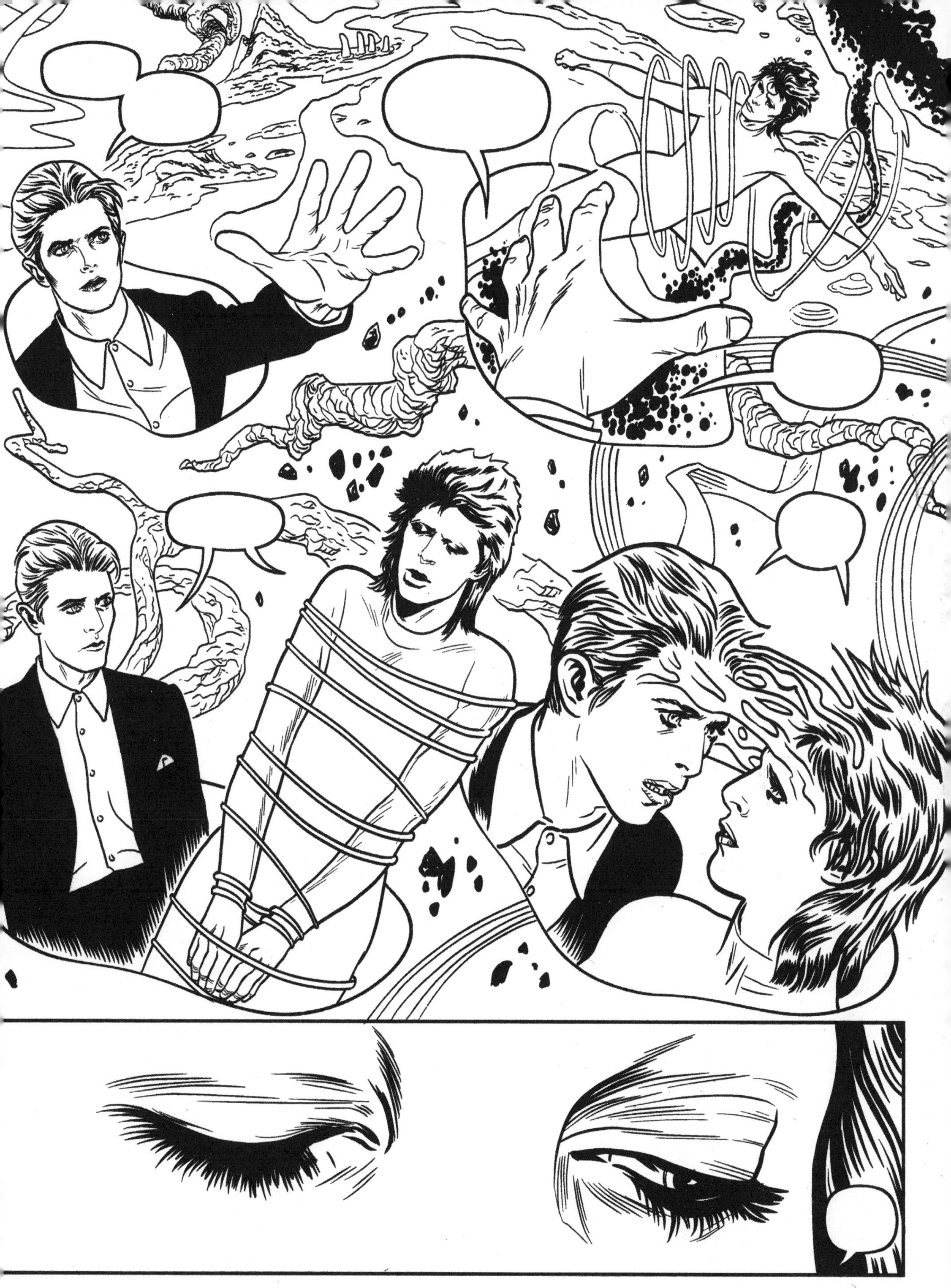

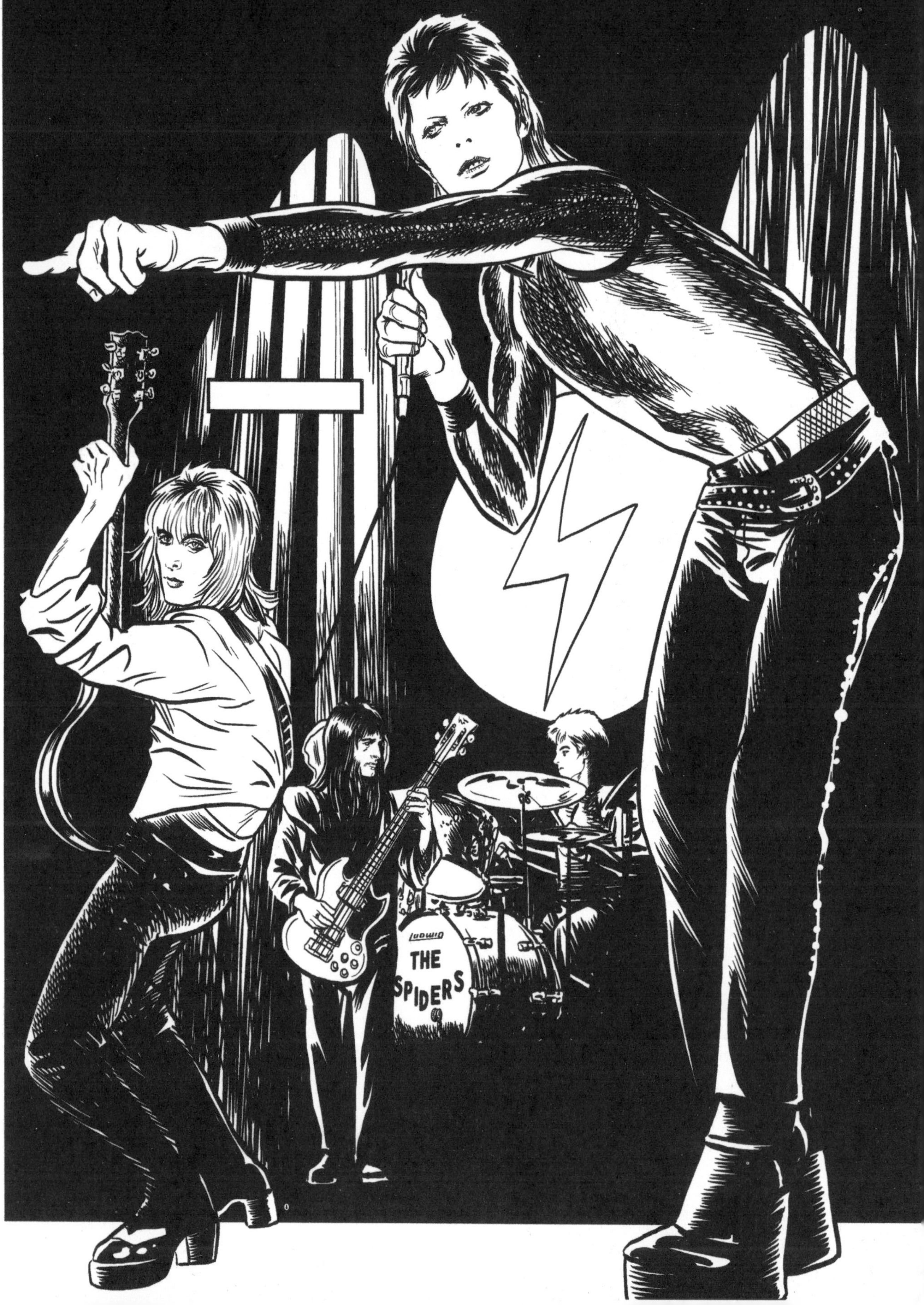
LUDWIG
THE SPIDERS

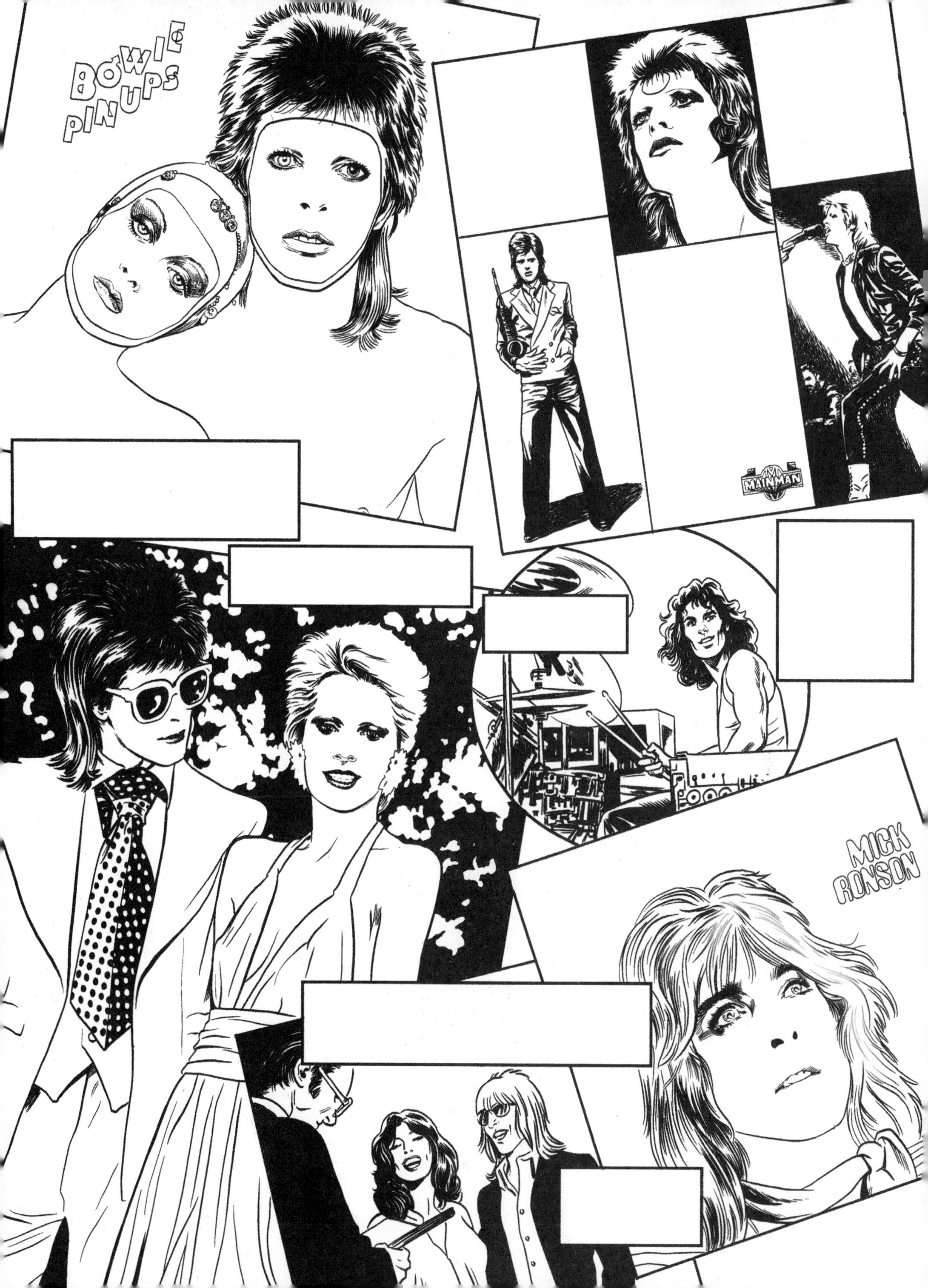
BOWIE PINUPS
MAINMAN
MICK RONSON

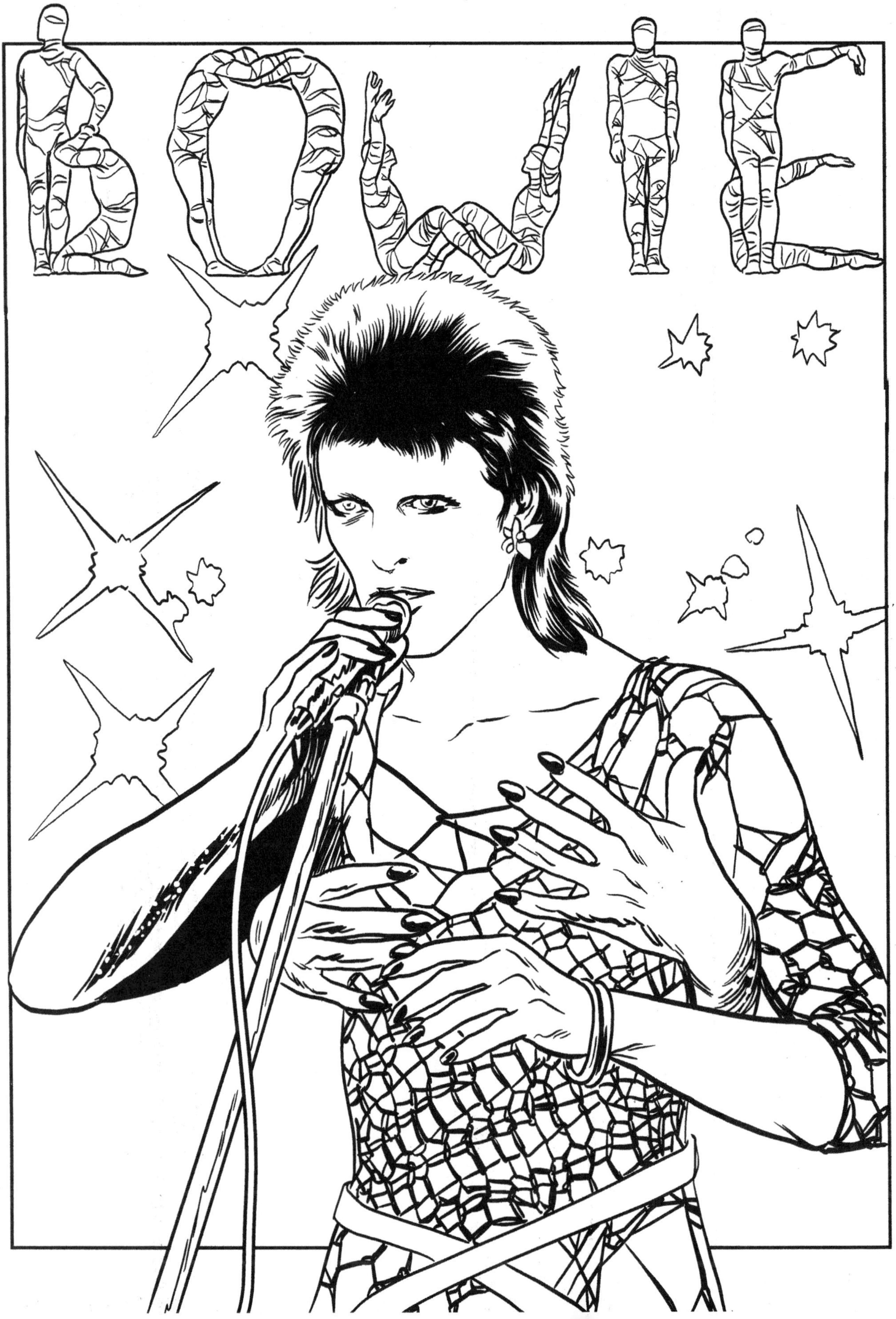
BOWIE

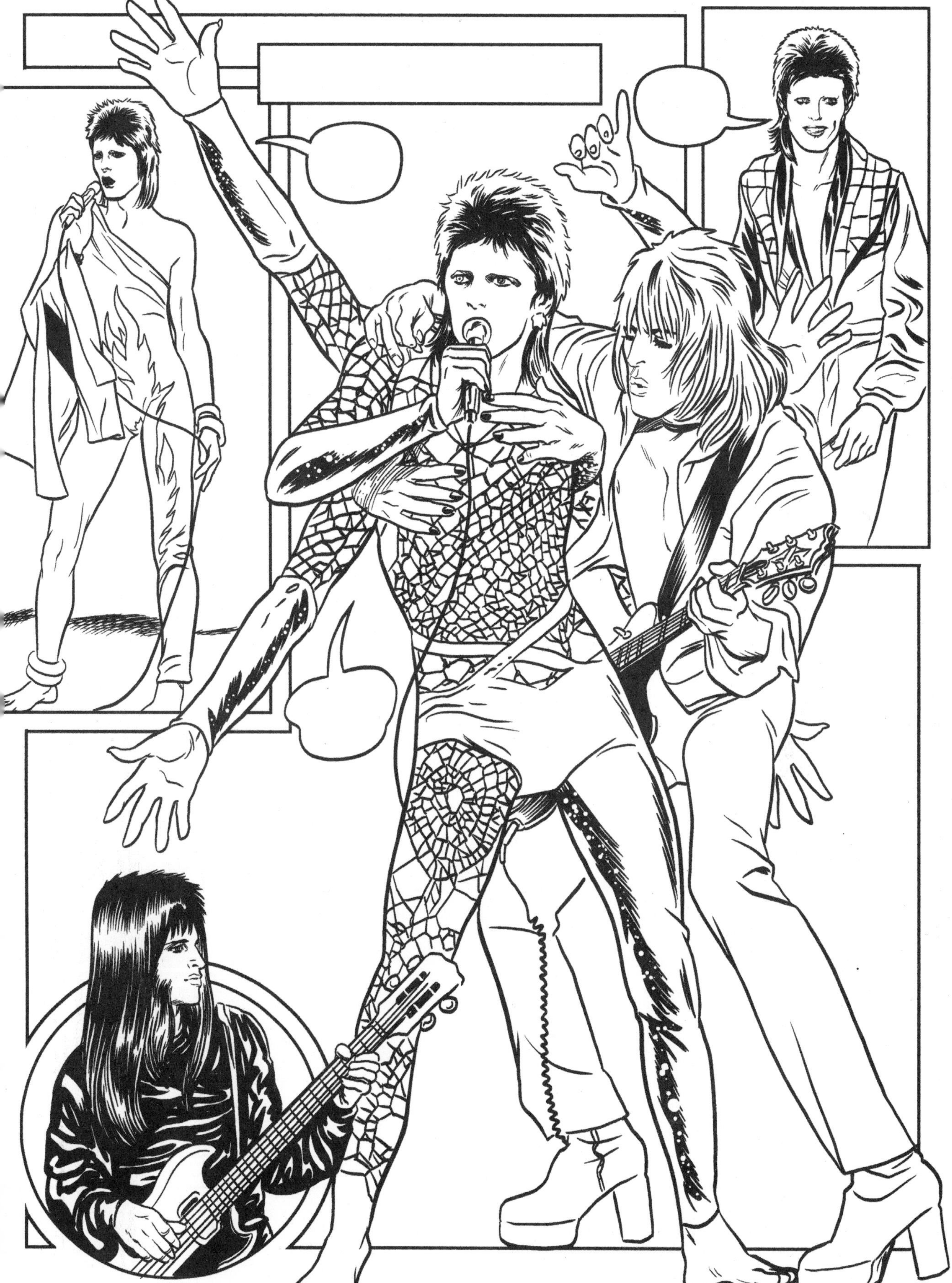

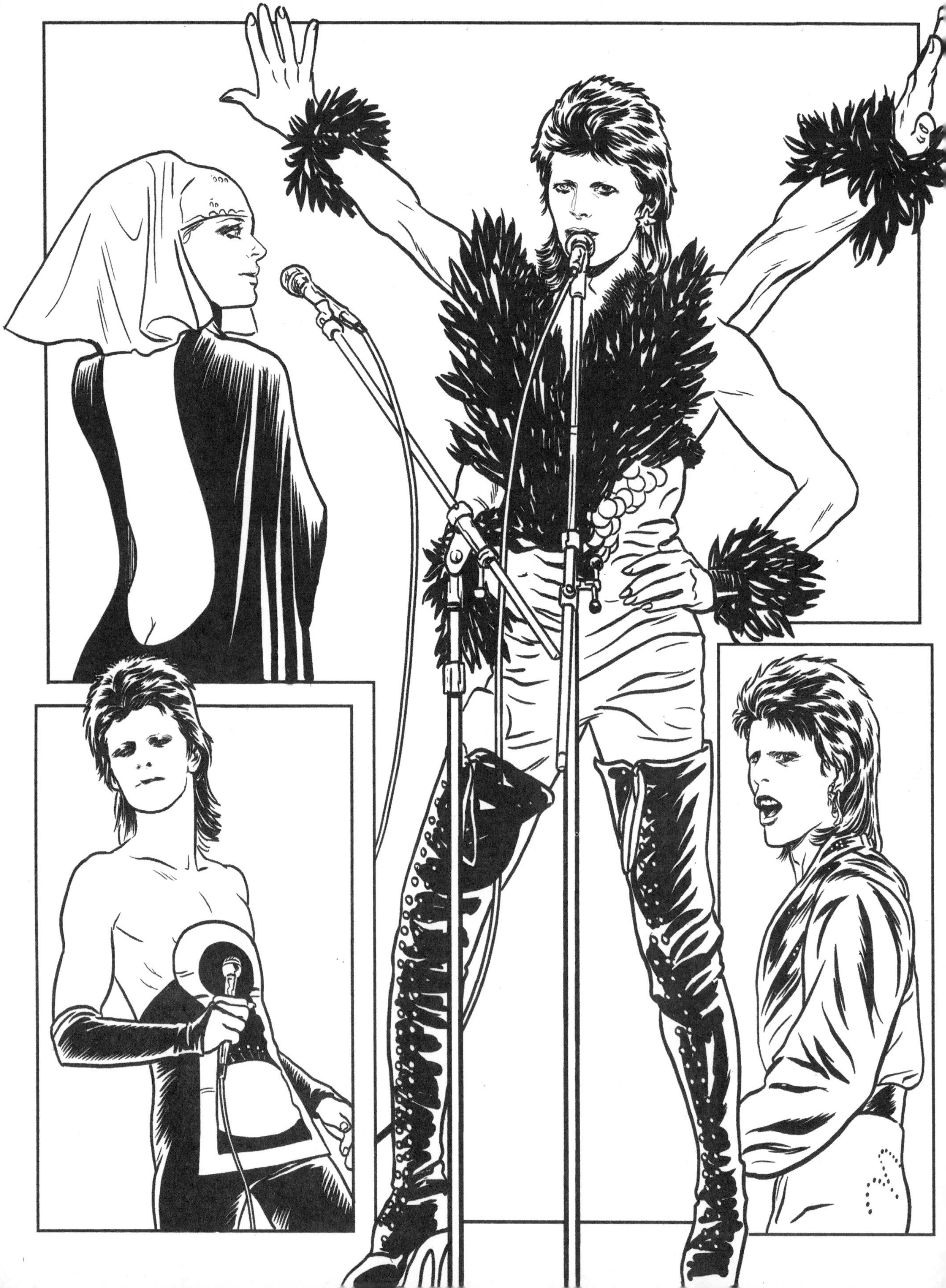

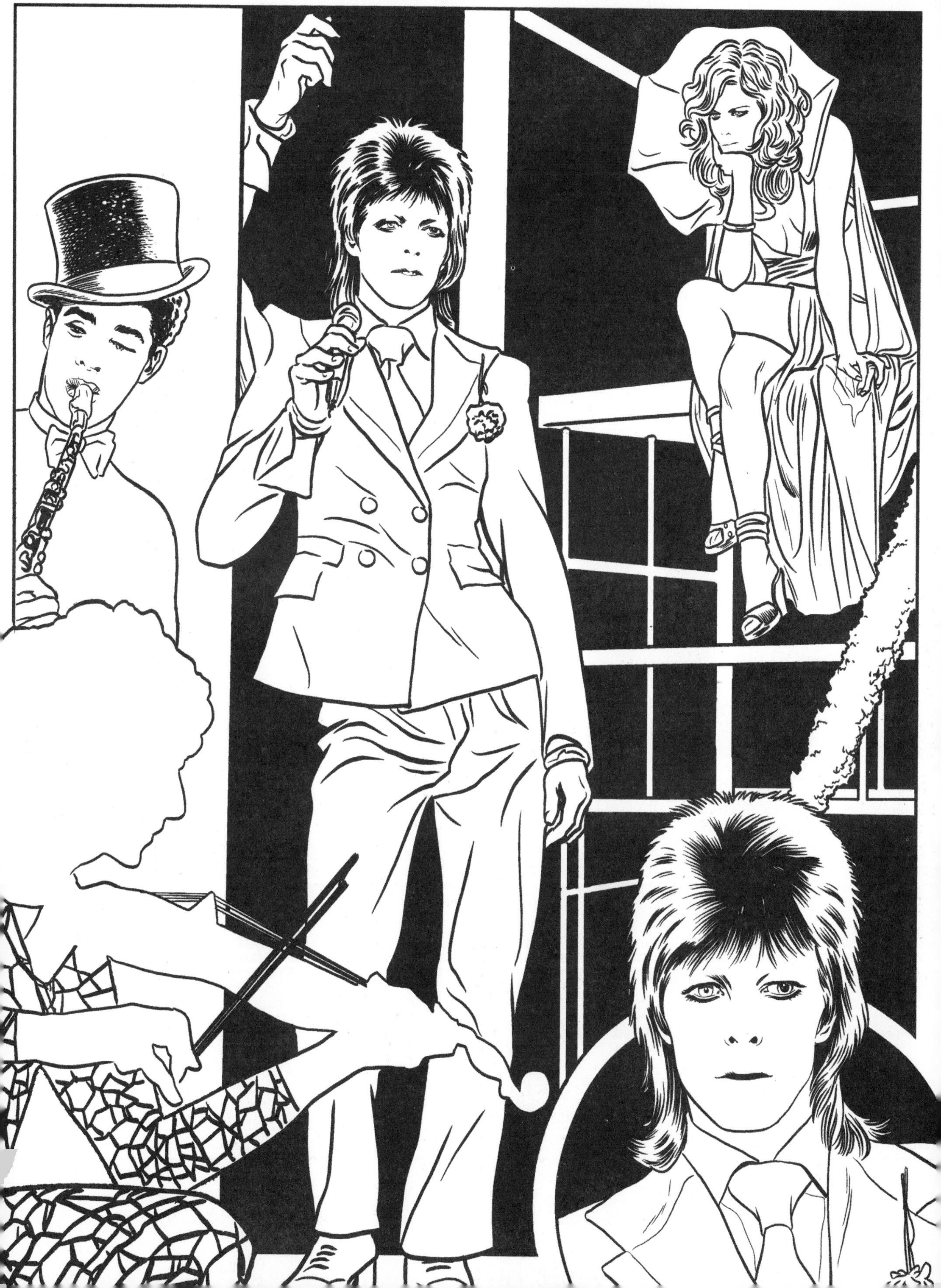

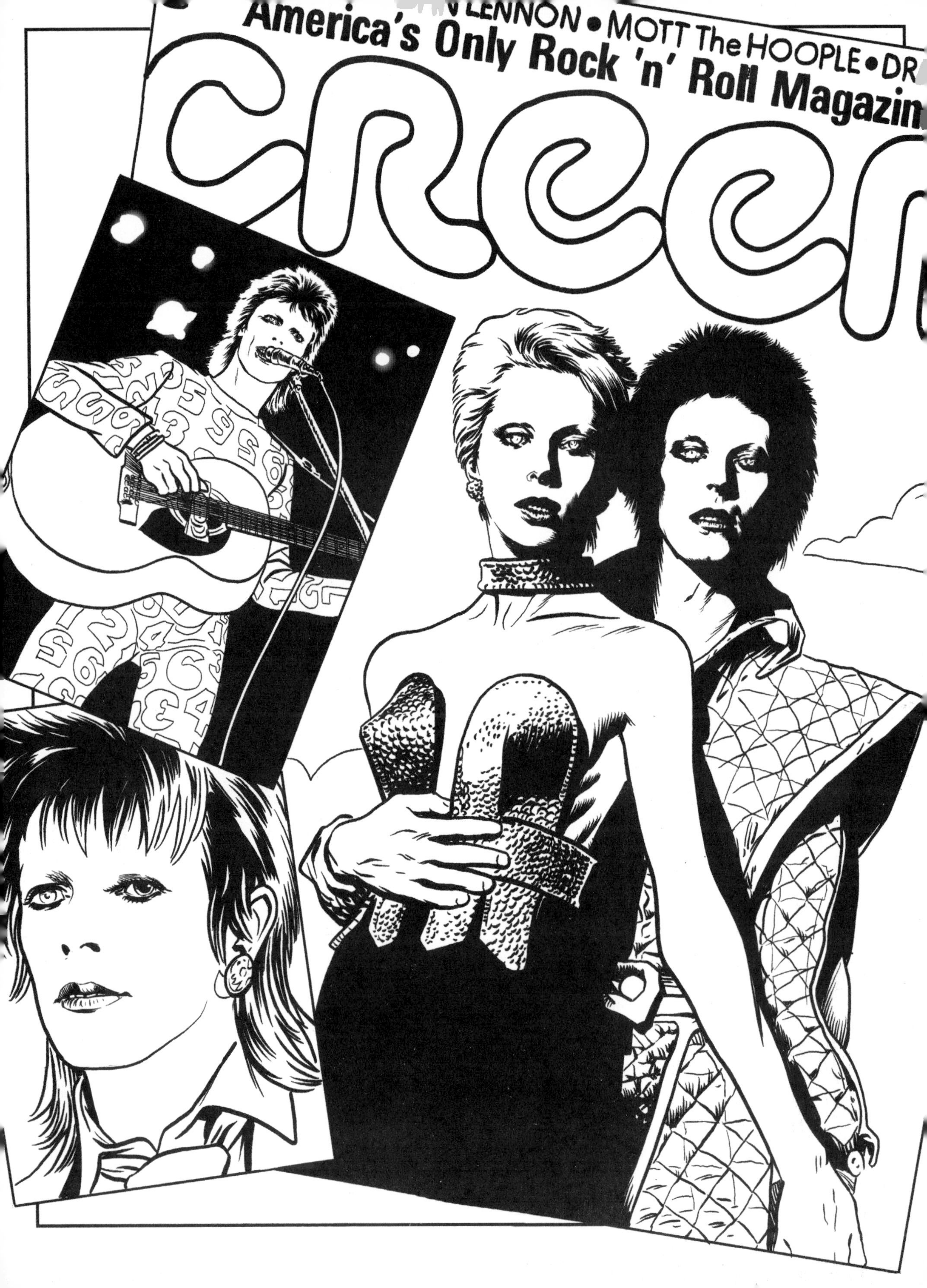
LENNON • MOTT The HOOPLE •
America's Only Rock 'n' Roll

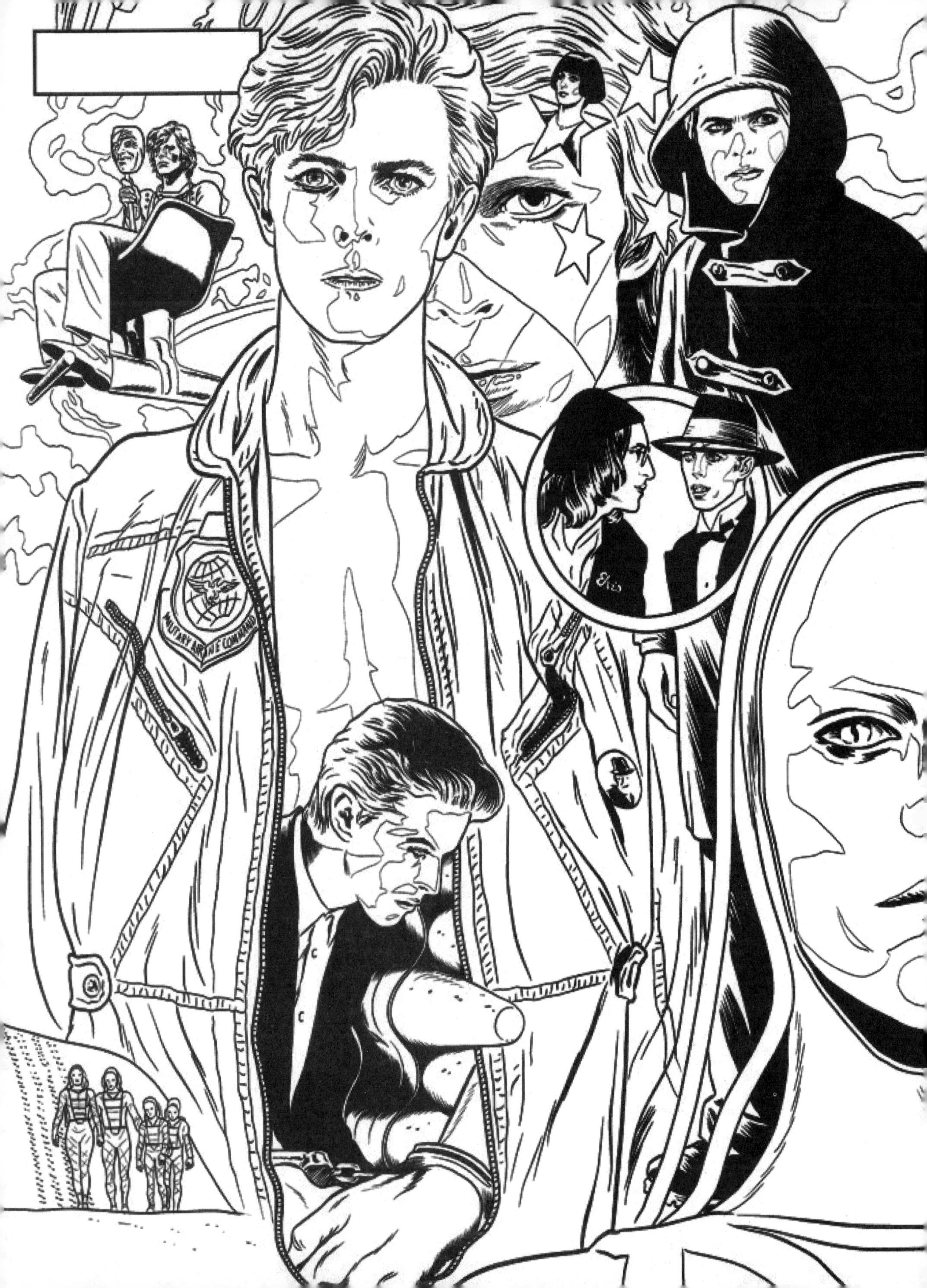

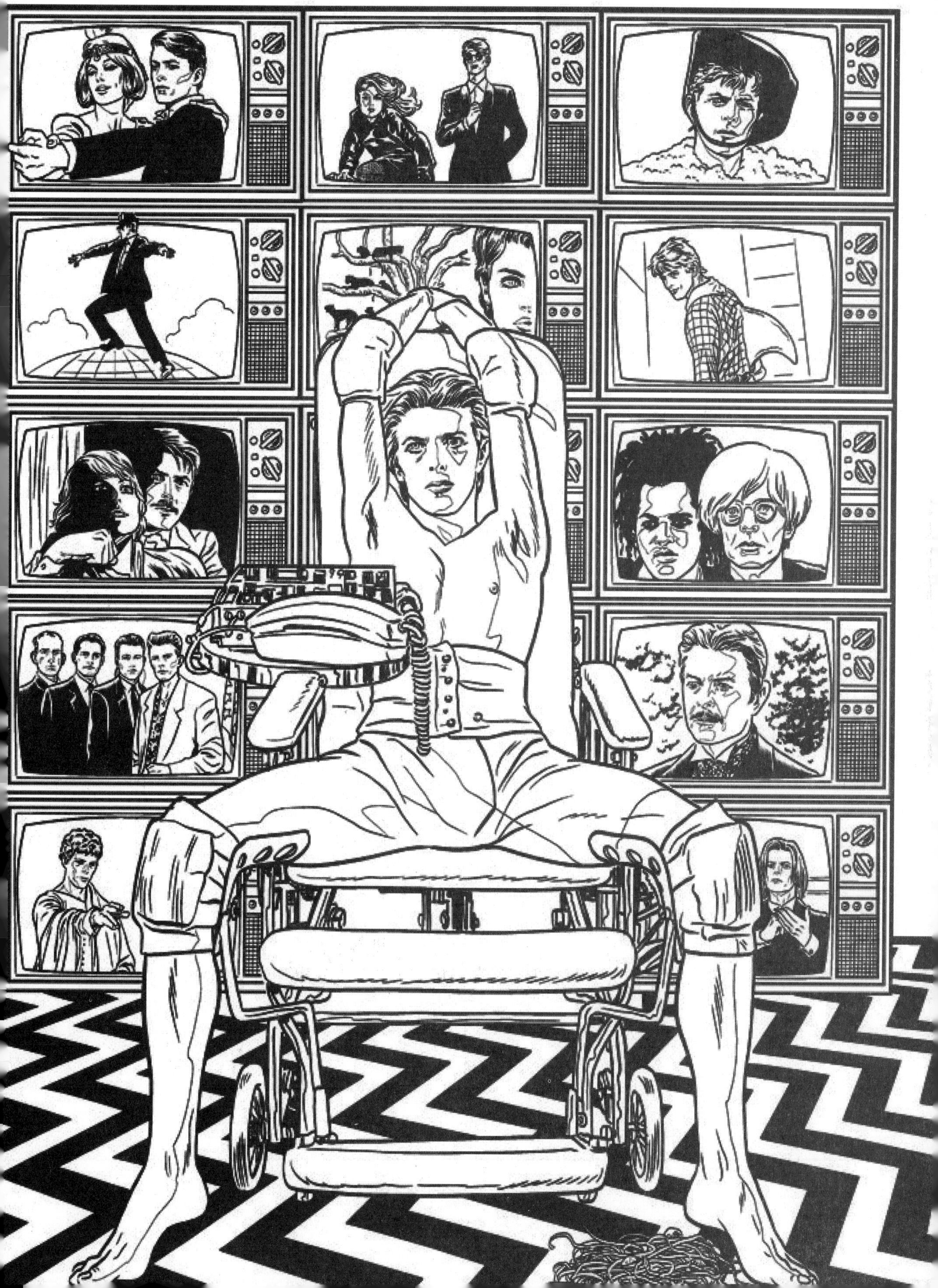

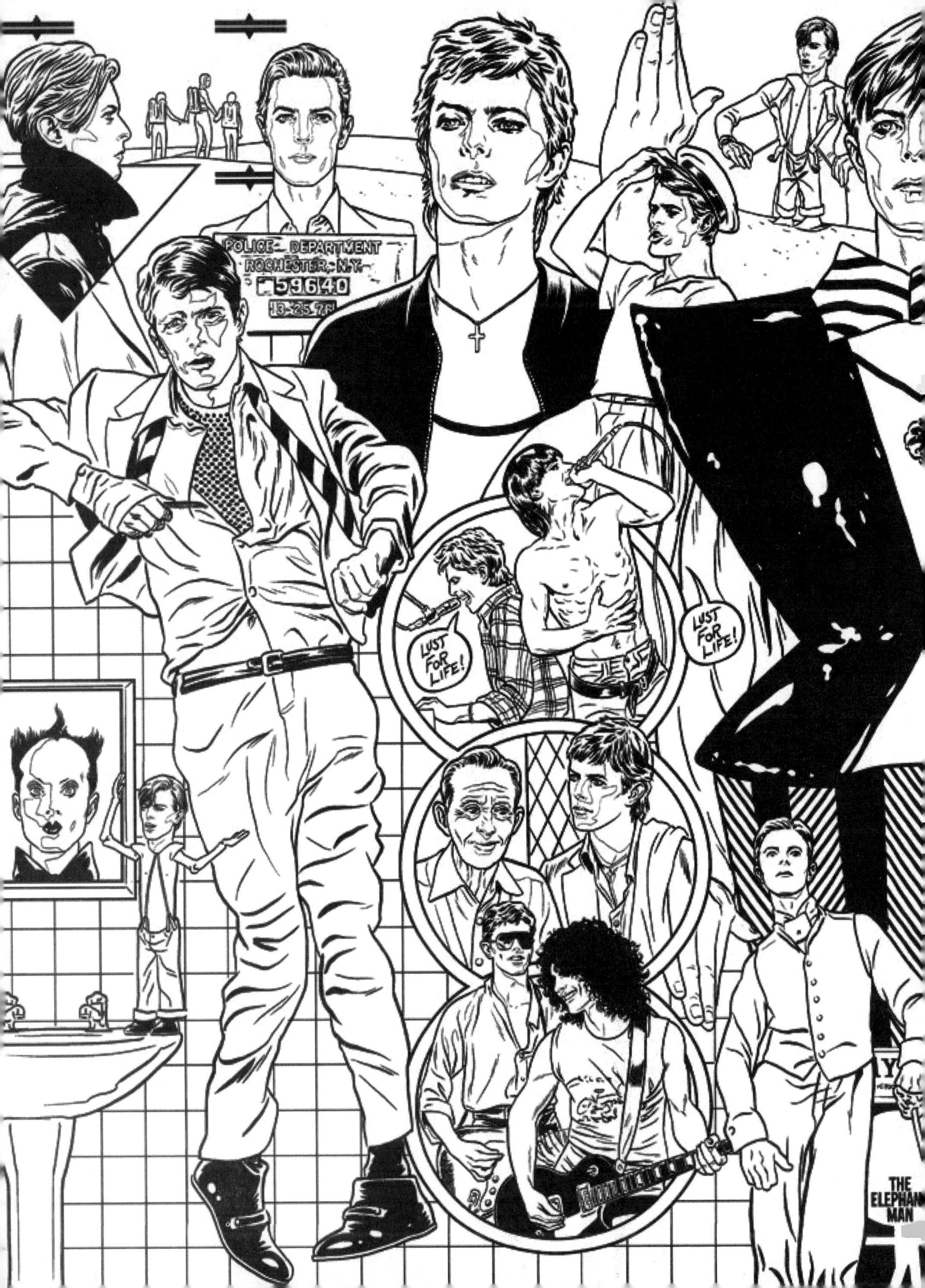
POLICE DEPARTMENT
ROCHESTER, N.Y.
59640
LUST FOR LIFE!
LUST FOR LIFE!
THE ELEPHAN
MAN

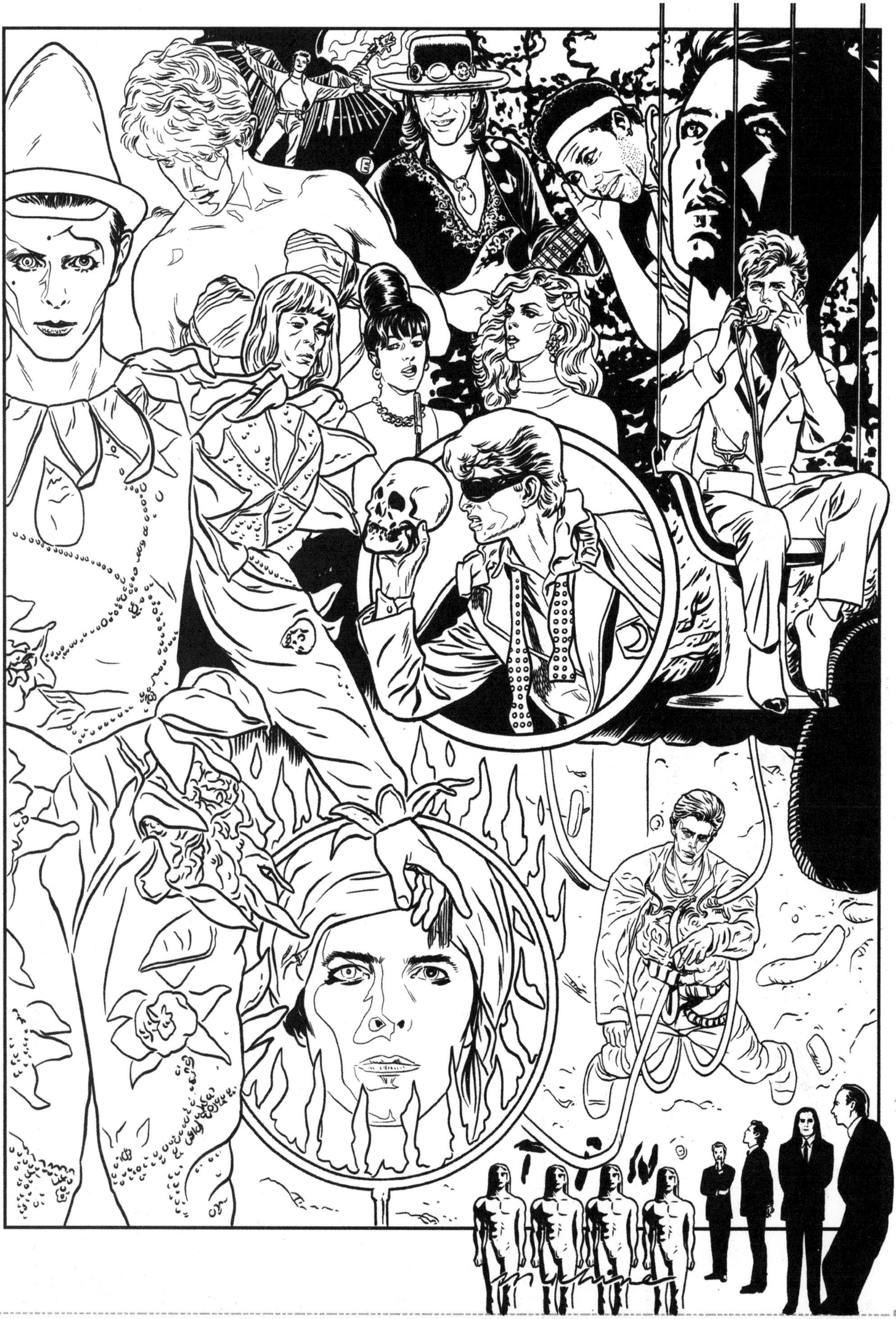

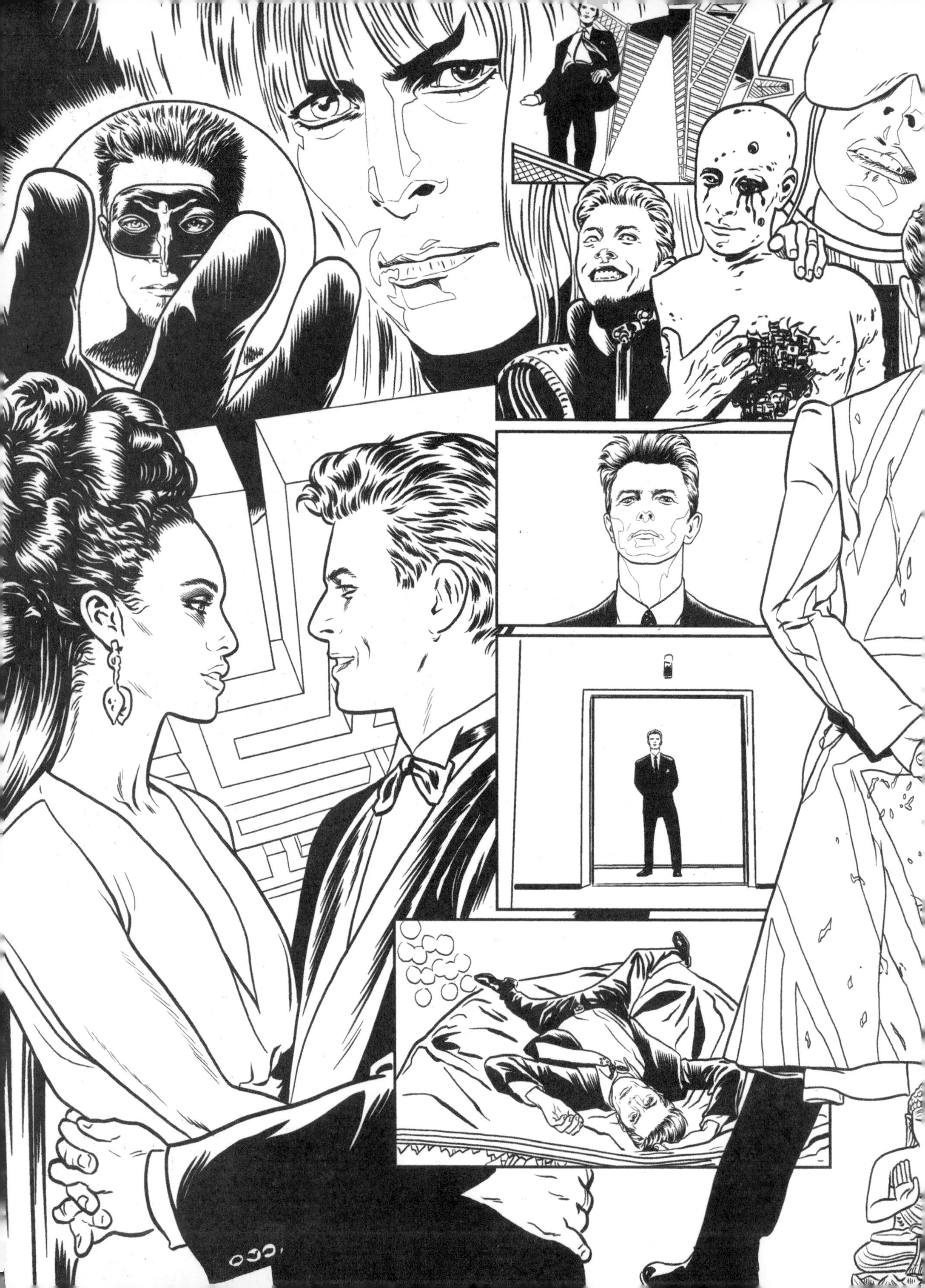

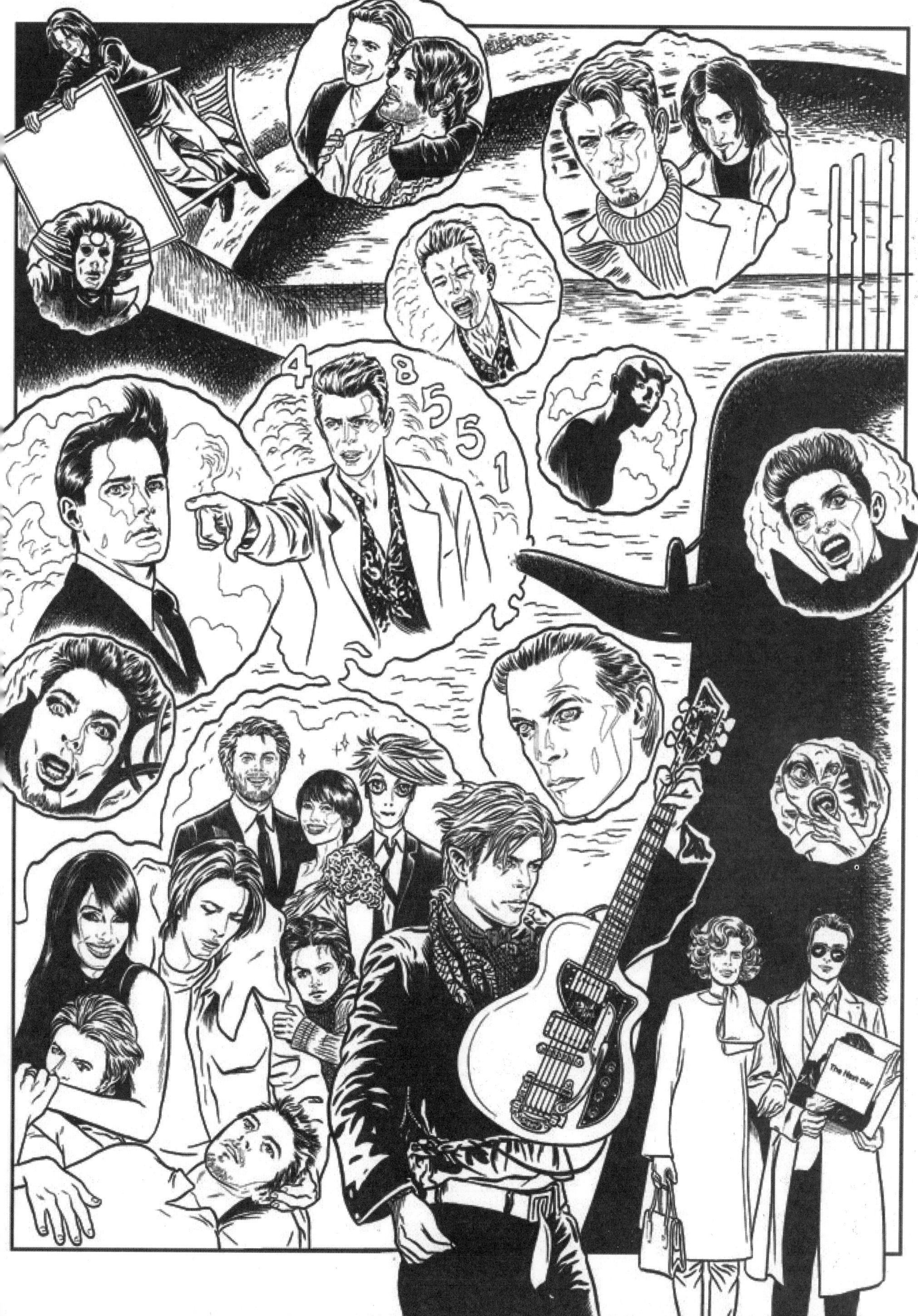
4 8 5 5 1
The Next Day

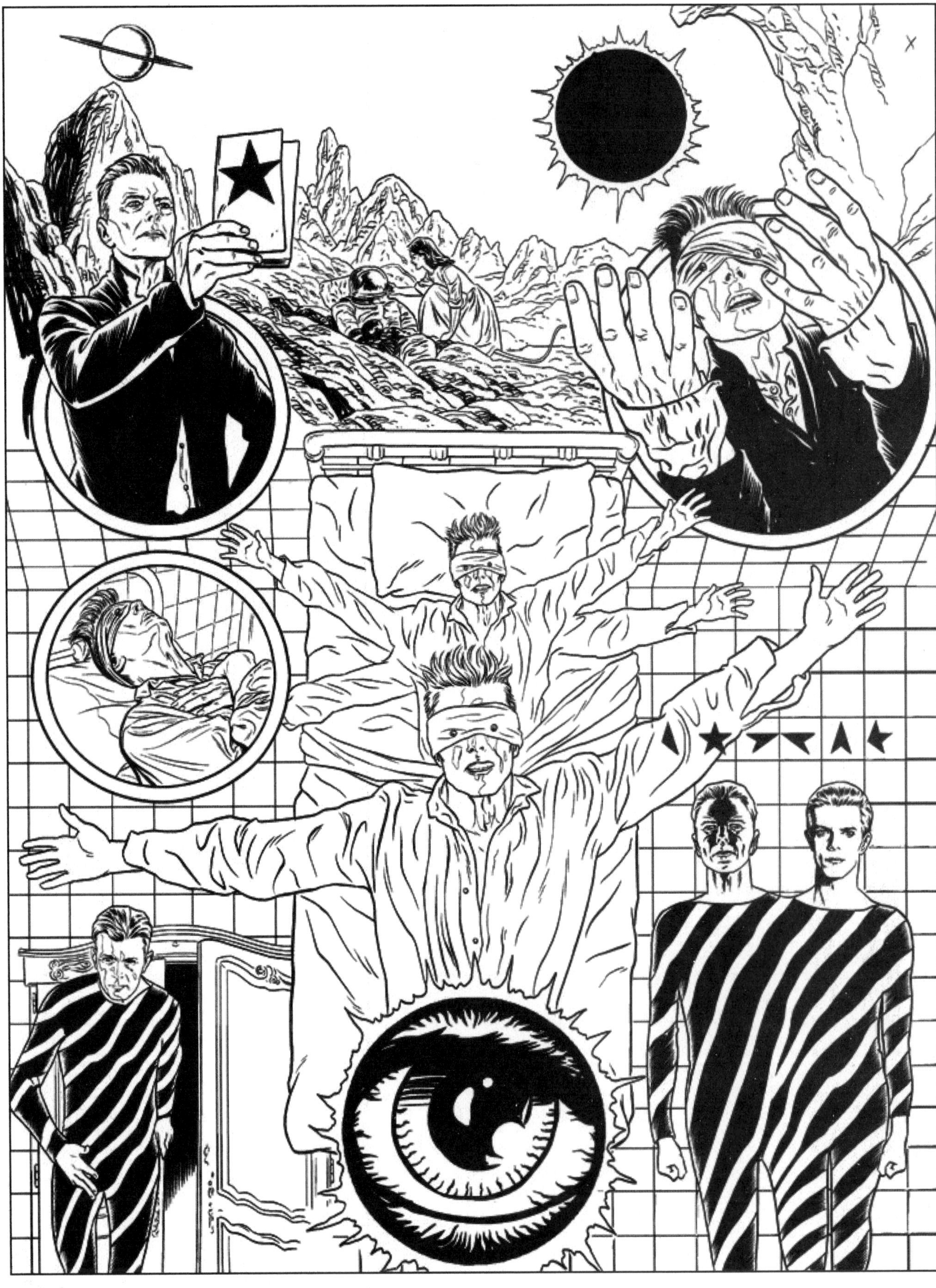

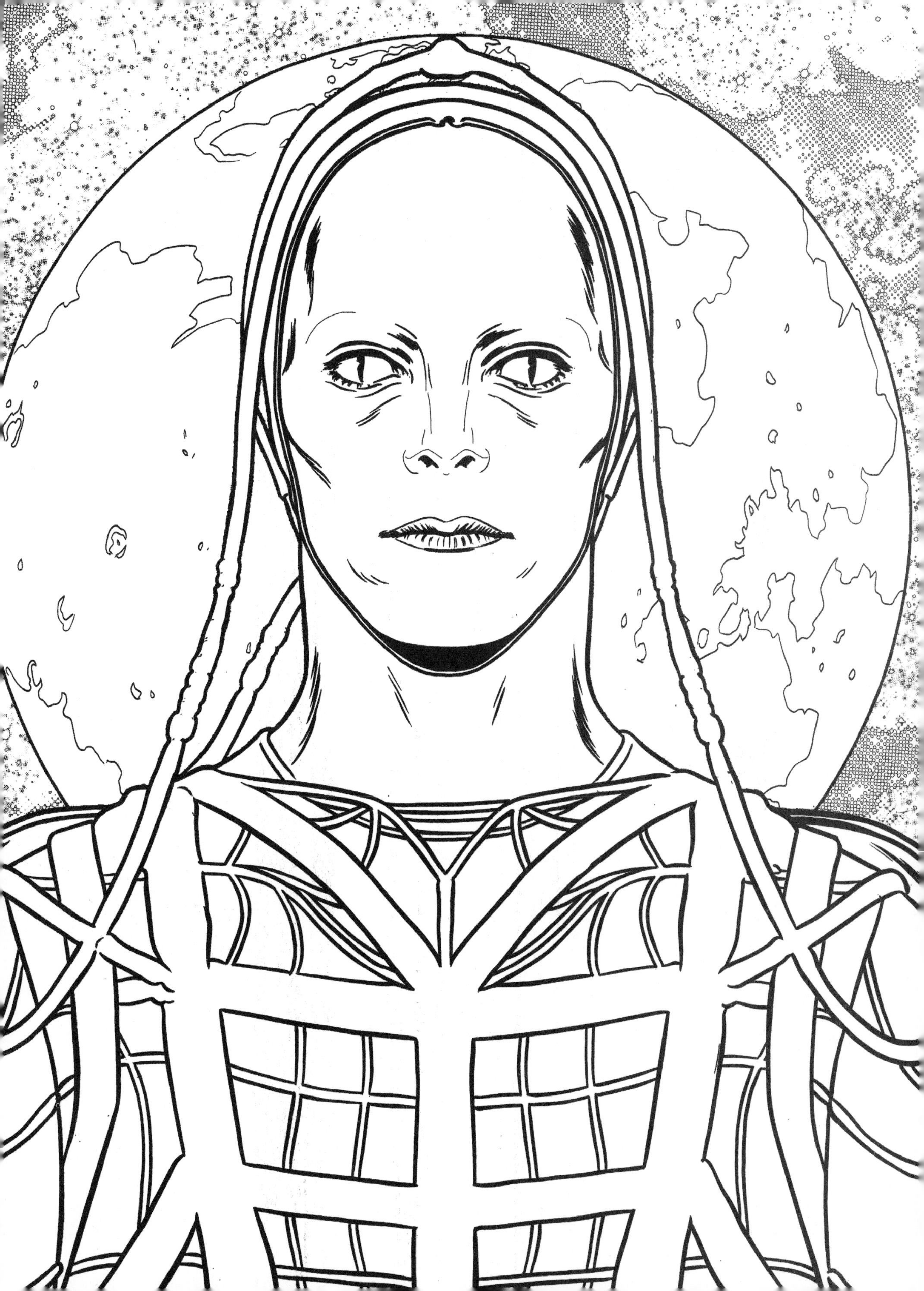

**INSIGHT
EDITIONS**

PO Box 3088
San Rafael, CA 94912
www.insighteditions.com

Find us on Facebook: www.facebook.com/InsightEditions
Follow us on Twitter: @insighteditions

Images from the Graphic Novel *BOWIE: Stardust, Rayguns & Moonage Daydreams* by Michael Allred, Steve Horton, and Laura Allred.

Published by Insight Editions, San Rafael, California, in 2020.

Library of Congress Cataloging-in-Publication Data available.

ISBN: 978-1-64722-217-8

Publisher: Raoul Goff
Associate Publisher: Vanessa Lopez
Creative Director: Chrissy Kwasnik
VP of Manufacturing: Alix Nicholaeff
Designer: Amy DeGrote
Associate Editor: Holly Fisher
Senior Production Editor: Elaine Ou
Production Associate: Eden Orlesky

ROOTS of PEACE   REPLANTED PAPER

Insight Editions, in association with Roots of Peace, will plant two trees for each tree used in the manufacturing of this book. Roots of Peace is an internationally renowned humanitarian organization dedicated to eradicating land mines worldwide and converting war-torn lands into productive farms and wildlife habitats. Roots of Peace will plant two million fruit and nut trees in Afghanistan and provide farmers there with the skills and support necessary for sustainable land use.

Manufactured in China by Insight Editions

10 9 8 7 6 5 4 3 2 1